PERIGEE

ACE

ALPHA

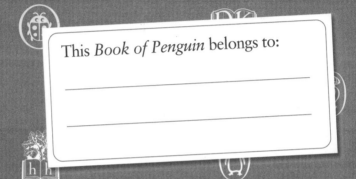

The
Penguin
Press

This *Book of Penguin* belongs to:

_____

_____

DK

VIKING

FIREBIRD

ROUGH
GUIDES

DUTTON

BERKLEY

RIVERHEAD
BOOKS

PENGUIN
FIG TREE

PENGUIN
MICHAEL
JOSEPH

celebra

NAL

PENGUIN BOOKS

Published by the Penguin Group
Penguin Books Ltd, 80 Strand, London WC2R ORL, England
Penguin Group (USA) Inc., 375 Hudson Street, New York NY10014, USA
Penguin Group (Canada), 90 Eglinton Avenue East, Suite 700, Toronto, Ontario M4P 2Y3, Canada
(a division of Pearson Penguin Canada Inc.)
Penguin Ireland, 25 St Stephen's Green, Dublin 2, Ireland,
(a division of Penguin Books Ltd)
Penguin Group (Australia), 250 Camberwell Road, Camberwell, Victoria 3124, Australia
(a division of Pearson Australia Group Pty Ltd)
Penguin Books India Pvt Ltd, 11 Community Centre, Panchsheel Park, New Delhi 110 017, India
Penguin Group (NZ), 67 Apollo Drive, Rosedale, North Shore 0632, New Zealand
(a division of Pearson New Zealand Ltd)
Penguin Books (South Africa) (Pty) Ltd, 24 Sturdee Avenue, Rosebank, Johannesburg 2196, South Africa

Penguin Books Ltd
Registered Offices: 80 Strand, London WC2R ORL, England
www.penguin.com

First published 2009
1

ISBN: 978–0–141–04335 –7

Written by Duncan Campbell-Smith and Penguin
Designed by Radley Yeldar. Illustrated by Heather Briggs and Robert Riche. Typeset in Sabon
Printed in England by CTD, on Skye Uncoated Brilliant White from McNaughton Paper

The
Book
of
Penguin

The Book of Penguin
What's inside?

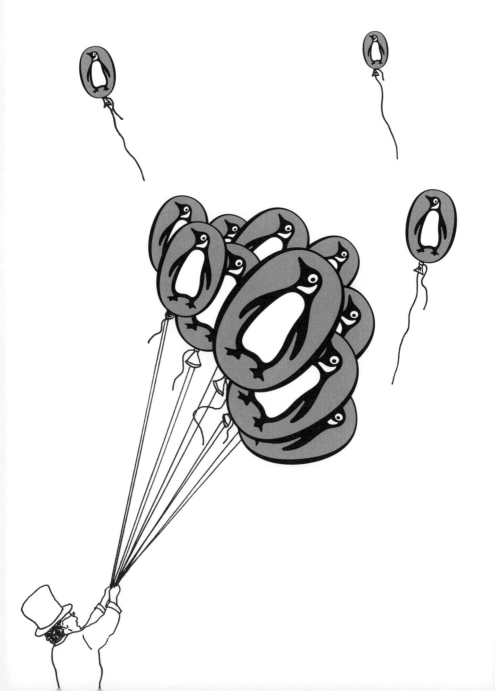

1

The bird takes flight

Introduction

Allen Lane, the founder of Penguin, published a series of short books in the 1940s offering practical guidance on everything from rabbit farming to the repair of electrical appliances. He called them Penguin Handbooks. *The Book of Penguin* is a handbook with a different purpose. It is short, like its predecessors, and is designed to be practical. It won't help you to breed a rabbit or change a plug, but we hope that people who care about Penguin – our authors, employees and readers, among others – will find it a useful guide to today's Penguin; what it stands for and where it's going.

It is, quite deliberately, a book, and not a website, blog or podcast. We need no convincing of the opportunity that digital technology presents to develop new kinds of content and to engage in a closer relationship with our readers. More of that later. But we want, in this slim volume, to celebrate the durable appeal of the physical book. As we survey the war zones in other media markets, it is encouraging to report that publishers are publishing, and readers are buying, more books than ever before. All over the world.

Physical books keep selling because they are desirable. Readers buy them not just for what's written between the covers, but because they are well designed and look good on a table or a shelf. Most people hate throwing books away, but they like to give, share and even to smell them. No mainstream consumer product is as collectable and durable as the book. We throw away our newspapers and magazines after we've read them, we walk round to the DVD rental store to find our next movie, and we download our music from iTunes. But we still go out (or stay in) and buy a book.

S o this is the first premise of *The Book of Penguin*. The physical book is in the best of health (and it's our obligation as publishers to keep it that way). The second premise is perhaps a little self-regarding, but we wouldn't be publishing this book unless we believed it. Penguin is special. It is special, most visibly, because of the extraordinary power of our brand. It is the most recognized and authoritative publishing brand in the world, but beyond that it is the only global consumer brand in any medium that represents intellectual and creative excellence. That's a bold claim, and we're ready to be proved wrong, but we can't think of another name that comes close.

Great brands cannot achieve their supremacy without the support of gifted designers and marketing professionals. Look at Apple, Google or Nike. But, in order to endure, these brands must also stand for something and engage the emotions of the consumer. Penguin does that. The bird in the oval represents an assurance of integrity and quality to readers around the world.

'A Penguin book should be, quite simply, a good book, whatever its content or format.'

That's a bit of a sweeping statement, we admit, and even our marketing department wouldn't argue that absolutely every book we've ever published meets that test. Sometimes we fail, but mostly we don't. The brand would soon be diminished if we did, and today it's stronger than ever. There will never be complete agreement about what sets Penguin apart. Design is certainly an important element; so too is a perception of value for money, dating back to the launch of the sixpenny paperback in 1935. Penguin has always published serious writing, but has never taken itself too seriously. It's a jaunty bird.

You may be thinking that we have this Penguin brand thing a little out of perspective. Some of our publishing imprints – Dorling Kindersley and Rough Guides, for example – have no perceptible connection with the Penguin name, while many of our most distinguished literary imprints have glorious independent pedigrees that stretch back further than Penguin itself. Putnam, a Penguin company in the US, sells more books than any other publishing imprint in America and traces its lineage to the foundation of a publishing partnership by George Palmer Putnam and John Wiley in 1838. Moreover, while Dorling Kindersley and Rough Guides rely on the strength of their own brand identities to sell their books, Penguin mostly depends on the reputation of its authors. We're under no illusion that Patricia Cornwell crime thrillers or Jamie Oliver cookbooks sell in their millions just because they are published by Penguin.

Yet it's Penguin that ties all this together. Not because it's the name of the company that manages all these imprints and publishes all these authors, though of course it is, but because the values and style of the organization shape our priorities and help determine our success as a publisher. That's why this is *The Book of Penguin*, and not *The Book of Putnam*, *The Book of DK* or *The Book of Puffin*, magical as all those names are.

Let's define this style in a little more depth. We are an international company. That is self-evident, perhaps, given that Penguin enjoys a leading position in every important market in the English-speaking world. But we're also international in outlook. The commercial centre of gravity of Penguin is in New York (we sell more than half our books in the US), but the heritage of Penguin itself is British. We have never had a dominant American or British culture and, from the earliest days, we have been comfortable investing in international markets. Putnam was the first US publishing house to establish an overseas operation, opening in London in 1841, while Allen Lane opened Penguin Inc. in New York just a few years after founding his business in London.

This outlook matters today more than ever. Here are three reasons (there are many more):

1 Thanks to digital technology a book can be created, stored, distributed or printed anywhere in the world at the press of a button. Geographic borders, which publishing companies have carefully delineated in protection of their right to publish a book in one territory or another, have less meaning in the digital world. Amazon and Google, to name but two, have the technical capacity to deliver the work of authors to almost anyone anywhere. Penguin's global structure enables it to pursue a conversation with these companies in a seamless way anywhere in the world.

2 English-language education is creating millions of potential Penguin customers every year in Asia alone. Penguin had the foresight to build a business in India almost two decades before our principal international competitors, and now we are reaping the rewards. Since then Penguin India has grown at an average annual rate of about 20 percent and we hope to maintain that momentum. The emerging markets of Asia and Africa represent a huge opportunity for international publishers, if they understand how to grasp it.

3 We've always assumed that the mature markets of Europe and North America would pioneer new developments in publishing. Not any more. If you want to understand how young people are reading (and writing) books using new technology don't just focus on London and New York. Head to Beijing or Seoul. We'll soon need to understand these consumers, and be selling to them, if we're to stay competitive in our heartland.

We're a company that believes in books and authors. Another truism, maybe, but remember that Penguin is part of Pearson, the biggest book publisher in the world (twice as big as its closest peer). Most big book publishing companies are owned by diversified media conglomerates that generate the majority of their sales from movies or television or newspapers. Pearson has other sources of revenue, in newspapers and educational services for example, but it is books – consumer books and educational books – that define the company.

We have to be successful publishers if we're going to be successful at anything, and we know that any publishing company is only as good as the people it employs and the authors that it publishes. So we need to recruit and retain the very best talent, in all areas of the company, and attract the finest authors, if we're to flourish.

Does this really set us apart? We think so. Our authors understand the independence and integrity that have always characterized Penguin's publishing – this is the company that published *Ulysses, Lady Chatterley's Lover* and *Lolita*, despite the serious legal and public consequences. Our people understand our commitment to publishing and our determination to invest in the growth and diversity of our company.

W e're a company that's facing the future. And the future is digital, that's for sure. That's not an argument for eBooks over physical books. It's simply the recognition that digital technology changes everything about the publishing business. A book is created as a digital file and only becomes a physical product as the printing presses roll; it is stored in a digital warehouse, enabling it to be distributed anywhere in the world in the format of the consumer's choice. So, if a reader in Malaysia finds a book via a search engine and wants to buy it by the chapter, have it printed locally and each chapter sent as a weekly gift to his mum, technology can make this happen.

Digital technology is a huge opportunity for publishers, and for their authors, as long as the legal rights of the author are protected. It will be impossible for authors themselves, or for their agents, to police the boundaries of piracy and copyright infringement. Publishers will increasingly assume this responsibility, and in a borderless world it won't be easy. Only international publishers fluent in digital technology will stand any kind of chance.

So, we do think that Penguin is a special breed of bird, international in outlook, committed to its business, its authors and its people, and ready to invest in its future. We also believe – as a final premise – that Penguin matters. People who work at Penguin and who write for Penguin know that what they do is important. The books that we publish enrich the lives of millions of readers around the world. They make people laugh and cry and think. Just as Allen Lane would have wished.

John Makinson *Chairman and CEO, Penguin Group*

2
A novel history
Our history and heritage

These are exciting times in publishing, with opportunities at hand to break radically with many traditional practices of the past. No one would have relished them more than Penguin's founder, Allen Lane, and so his approach to publishing is a good place to start this overview of Penguin's business today. Penguin still has an Allen Lane imprint, but his legacy goes a lot deeper than that.

Allen Lane was a complicated man. Apparently he read very few books (from cover to cover, anyway). He had little interest in theatre or the arts, and none at all in music. He could be indecisive, had no aptitude whatsoever for numbers, and he hated paperwork and loathed meetings of any kind. Less surprising, on the other hand, was the catalogue of strengths that, together with a demonic energy, made him a formidable entrepreneur. He was utterly single-minded, he grasped even the tiniest details of his business and he had a shrewd eye for the next big opportunity. He took huge risks with great panache, he could be extraordinarily persuasive and he consistently inspired a coterie of brilliant people to work for him.

L ane had what one of Penguin's first editors described as the 'gift of curiosity'. He asked questions of everyone he met, and was invariably an attentive listener: he was an obsessive gleaner of information on every topic of the day. Perhaps it was this habit of mind, above all others, that made him a great publisher. In the business of sniffing things out, Lane had few equals.

What he sniffed out in the mid 1930s was the potential demand in England for quality books at low prices. He did not invent the paperback – it had a history dating back to the nineteenth century. And within recent years a German publisher had reworked the format for a mass-market audience, in ways that Lane – who had been working for a small London publisher since leaving school in 1919 – certainly noted. Drawing on his knowledge of the UK trade, though, Lane hit on the idea of books with a truly original three-in-one combination.

'Allen Lane should be regarded as the greatest educative communicator of our time... whose contribution to the printed word has never been surpassed.'
Sir Robert Lusty *Journalist and publisher (1909 – 91)*

F irst, they would be cheap enough, as he would say, to be 'bought as easily and casually as a packet of cigarettes'. Second, they would always consist of quality titles, albeit to suit a wide range of reading tastes. Third, and in retrospect most remarkably, they would be promoted from the outset in line with the advertising industry's latest and fanciest notions of 'consumer marketing'. They would be given a brand name and be packaged attractively enough to be sold as items that bookish people might collect.

Off to a memorable start

How Allen Lane turned this vision into a successful business is, of course, part of British publishing folklore. The old chestnuts start with the birth of the concept, as the exasperated young publisher finds himself stranded on a railway platform and searching the station kiosk in vain for anything of interest to read. Then comes the brainstorming session to pick an imprint title, at which various bird names are in the air when a secretary shouts out from behind a partition, 'What about penguins?' Cue for young office manager to be sent off to London Zoo with some petty cash to buy a sketchbook and try his hand at a suitable logo.

Next follow various stormy encounters between Lane and London's stuffy publishing establishment. His peers are convinced that he will bankrupt the whole trade with his

reckless plan to buy reprint rights and turn hardbacks into paperbacks at sixpence each. But George Orwell, as brutally honest as ever, agrees with Lane. He thinks paperbacks a splendid idea for readers: 'So splendid that if the other publishers had any sense they would combine against them and suppress them.'

They very nearly do just that, with a little help from the booksellers. Lane approaches a string of publishers about reprint rights. Most reject the idea out of hand. The retailers, meanwhile, either cold-shoulder it or suggest stocking the new format in bins outside the shop. Lane finds himself cast as the rebel outsider – which suits him just fine. He presses ahead, eventually managing to extract reprint rights for ten titles and he begins printing 20,000 copies of each.

To break even, he needs an average sale of around 18,000 books. The selling does not go well. In fact, after several weeks on the road, Lane and his small team win orders for just 7,000 of each title. Humiliation looms. Then, with days to go before publication, a disconsolate Lane calls on the haberdashery buyer of the Woolworths chain. This gentleman stocks just a small range of low-brow titles that sits beside the ribbons and the bows. But his wife takes a shine to the young salesman, so the buyer submits an order – for 63,500 copies, no less.

To everyone's amazement, they sell out within days of publication and Woolworths is soon back for many more. Other booksellers trip over themselves to catch up – and, from that moment, Lane never looks back. He sets up his own company, Penguin Books, in the derelict and mouse-infested crypt of a church in central London. A handful of staff work there surrounded by bricked-in coffins. New books from the printers are dropped down a makeshift chute from the graveyard. Once they hit the shops, though, sales soar – with three million books shipped in the first twelve months – and Penguin's rise to the top is unstoppable. At the first Frankfurt Book Fair after World War II, in 1949, no one is surprised to see Penguin as almost the only British trade publisher on parade. By the end of that decade, its turnover far exceeded that of any of London's hardback houses.

1935

The first ten Penguin paperbacks were published in 1935, sparking a paperback revolution. Book one was *Ariel* by André Maurois.

What they said...

'We believed in the existence in
this country of a vast reading public
for intelligent books at a low price,
and staked everything on it.'

Sir Allen Lane *Penguin founder*
(1902 – 70)

'If a book is any good,
the cheaper the better.'

Bernard Shaw *(1856 – 1950)*

'Few authors have ever had a
publisher they admire more than their
own books, or even themselves. I've said
it before, there's nothing like a Penguin.'

J. K. Galbraith *(1908 – 2006)*

'Splendid value for sixpence.
So splendid that if other publishers
had any sense they would combine
against them and suppress them.'

George Orwell *(1903 – 50)*

'These Penguin Books are
amazingly good value for money. If you
can make the series pay for itself, with
such books at such a price, you will have
performed a great publishing feat.'

J. B. Priestley *(1894 – 1984)*

1937

Launch of the Pelican imprint publishing original non-fiction books on contemporary issues.

1940

Puffin was born with a series of non-fiction picture books for children.

1946

Penguin Classics launched with the first title, Homer's *Odyssey*.

Right time, right idea

It's an astonishing story, spawning the kind of myths and legends that giant corporations rightly cherish as an antidote to modern uniformity. But how did it happen? Well, there could hardly have been a better time to launch cheap imprints. In addition to the demand for low-priced fiction, serious books about contemporary politics had an unprecedented appeal in the troubled years leading up to the Second World War.

The same was true in its aftermath, with the emergence of a far less deferential post-war society in which millions of British men and women had aspirations to educate themselves and to get ahead in life, as never before. And during the war itself, books were ordered in huge quantities for distribution to the armed services, with an 'A' format paperback for every khaki pocket. But Lane and a group of formidable colleagues rode their luck by responding to these opportunities with huge flair and – to employ a much overused word – creativity.

They seized every chance to nurture offshoots of the original paperback concept. To the mostly fiction list of Penguin was added an exclusively non-fiction imprint, called Pelican. To the growing stock of reprints was added a brilliant series of commissioned new titles, christened Penguin Specials. And even wartime logistics failed to deter them from launching a stream of new paperback series. These included Puffin Books for children, founded in 1940, and a brave foray into fresh translations of the non-English literary canon, which appeared from 1946 onwards as Penguin Classics.

S ales mounted steadily. From a newly built head office and warehouse at Harmondsworth, next to London's Heathrow airport, Penguin dispatched around five million books in 1950, with half going off to foreign markets, especially the US and Australia, where the company had set up local sales subsidiaries. Given the low cost of reprint licences and the (very) modest royalties acceptable to most of its commissioned non-fiction authors, the high volumes helped Penguin turn a real profit, despite its rock-bottom prices. With the apparent blessing of its hardback peers – several of whom, including Hamish Hamilton and Michael Joseph, joined together in a group agreement to give Penguin the right of first refusal on paperback rights to all their titles – it had carved out a briefly uncontested space in a booming market.

'We aimed at making something pretty smart, a product clean and as bright as two pins, modern enough not to offend the fastidious high-brow, and yet straightforward and unpretentious.'
Jan Tschichold *Penguin designer in the late 1940s*

Penguin had established itself as far more than a national monopoly, though. It had made itself into a national institution. The monopoly disappeared, as it was bound to, once other publishers started waking up in the 1950s to the idea of having their own paperbacks. However, the iconic status of Penguin, and the instant appeal of its brand to the reading public, remained in place – and even by 1950 it was deeply enough rooted to have survived to this day.

Growing pains

We need to fast-forward over much that happened in the next couple of decades. Penguin went on innovating, with the launch of new imprints such as Peregrine and Penguin Modern Classics, both begun in 1961; by reviving others, such as Pelican and Penguin Specials, which had lain dormant for a while; by introducing new genres to the mass market, including a cookery list that included five Elizabeth David titles by 1964; and by building Puffin Books, under former magazine editor Kaye Webb, into the undisputed champion among UK children's paperback imprints. By the mid 1950s Penguin had already doubled unit sales since 1950 – with the split between UK and overseas sales remaining, as for many years to come, at around 50:50 – and sales had tripled by the end of the 1960s.

Naturally all this transformed the finances of the company – though none of its bold new imprints ever had quite as dramatic an impact on Penguin as a solitary title that appeared in Great Britain in 1960. This was D.H. Lawrence's *Lady Chatterley's Lover*, which famously encountered a spot of bother at the Old Bailey on its way into the high-street bookshops. Penguin was charged under the Obscene Publications Act and was later acquitted.

The publicity around the case helped Penguin sell two million copies of the book in the six weeks leading up to Christmas 1960. Months later, when Lane and his fellow shareholders sold the company on the public market, the stock was 150 times oversubscribed, a new record for the London Stock Exchange.

New ownership

In 1967 Penguin made its first sally into hardback publishing, with the launch of Allen Lane The Penguin Press. Around this time, Lane was becoming increasingly interested in

1967

Imprint Allen Lane The Penguin Press founded – a new venture for Penguin that allowed it to publish in both hardback and paperback.

educational publishing. It seemed to him a natural progression for the publisher of Penguin Classics. A few fledgling projects were launched but, in reality, as a trade publisher, Penguin simply didn't have the necessary management resources. The issue was resolved by an approach from Longman, which had itself been taken over in 1968 by S. Pearson & Son Ltd, the owner of the *Financial Times*, and the predecessor to today's Pearson plc. The merged company, Pearson Longman, at least offered the prospect of some future dovetailing of trade and educational publishing. And, in the meantime, it gave lavish assurances that Penguin's operating autonomy as a trade house would be fully respected. Allen Lane died in July 1970, and Pearson Longman's acquisition of Penguin was announced the next day.

1970

S. Pearson & Son Ltd, the predecessor to global media group Pearson, acquires Penguin.

PEARSON

The 1970s provided a tough economic climate for Penguin and the book trade at large. But while Penguin's adult publishing rather lost its way, children's books came to the rescue. Kaye Webb was now presiding over a juvenile list that was like no other. Blockbusters such as Roald Dahl's *Charlie and the Chocolate Factory* and Richard Adams's *Watership Down* (which would go on to become one of Penguin's bestselling fiction titles in any category) kept the red ink at bay. The decade also saw two significant events which were to define the direction of the modern company. A top American hardback house, The Viking Press, was acquired in 1975 (more on this in a moment), then, late in 1978, it was announced that an American paperback publisher had been appointed as Penguin's chief executive – Peter Mayer.

Peter was to stay with Penguin for the next eighteen years. His was to be an exciting era that restored much of the flair and sheer unpredictability that had marked the best years under Allen Lane. He physically relocated the creative departments from Harmondsworth to offices in central London, and he also set about relocating the focus of the firm's creative mindset. Instead of relying on its unparalleled backlist and a narrow range of frontlist titles that might (or might not) throw up an occasional bestseller, Peter decreed that Penguin should put all the power of its brand behind frontlist marketing, which would ensure a dozen or two big titles every year. The first campaigns were launched within a matter of months, with the full-scale promotion of a romantic novel that was published in hardback the previous year by Allen Lane: M.M. Kaye's *The Far Pavilions*.

Frontlist marketing

M.M. Kaye's *The Far Pavilions* was the first of Penguin's new blockbuster titles in 1978.

In August 1960, after the ban on *Lady Chatterley's Lover* was lifted, there were many stories of customers buying the book and burning it in the street.

Of course, such stories only ignited sales of the book further, resulting in Penguin shifting over two million copies in the six weeks following the trial.

'There are worse crimes than burning books. Not reading them is one.' Joseph Brodsky

Compensating for the decline of the old business model would mean a range of new tactics, as Peter appreciated from the start. More aggressive marketing of commercial titles became a hallmark of the 1980s. Where *The Far Pavilions* had led the way, with sales of 300,000 copies in six months, many others followed, including Shirley Conran's *Lace* and Celia Brayfield's *Pearls*. More imaginative repackaging of backlist titles was another priority, so the traditional 'A' format was replaced by the slightly larger 'B' format. And every opportunity was taken to make Penguin's frontlist once again the talking point of the book trade.

1983

Acquired Frederick Warne, best known for its Beatrix Potter titles.

I n another echo of the best Lane years, Mayer also gathered around him a distinguished team of UK editors, who between them built up an extraordinary list of authors. And in a flurry of activity between 1983 and 1985, three new businesses were acquired – Frederick Warne, Hamish Hamilton and Michael Joseph. Frederick Warne brought the *Peter Rabbit* children's books to Penguin, which turned out to be no small nugget of pure gold. The other two purchases, along with a newly created Viking UK imprint, greatly expanded Penguin's presence in hardback publishing. Like its competitors, who had moved in the opposite direction by adding new paperback imprints to their in-house hardback portfolio, Penguin had now fully come to terms with the commercial necessity of 'vertical publishing'.

Changing direction

Mayer travelled the globe tirelessly. In addition to overseeing Penguin's local companies in Australia (founded, in a never-to-be-forgotten tin shed, in 1946), New Zealand (founded in 1973) and Canada (founded in 1974), he set up new companies in both India (founded in 1987) and South Africa (founded in 1989). And, as we'll see, there was much to keep him busy in New York too.

1988

Published Salman Rushdie's *The Satanic Verses*.

The late 1980s marked the start of a difficult era for Penguin, epitomized perhaps by the extraordinary security crisis that followed the 1988 publication of Salman Rushdie's *The Satanic Verses* – with the Ayatollah Khomeini's fatwa following months later, in February 1989. But they were also years of achievement. Penguin was still capable of taking the market by surprise with brilliant marketing coups, never more so than in 1995 when the miniature Penguin 60s were published to celebrate the firm's sixtieth birthday.

Penguin 60s

Published to celebrate the firm's sixtieth birthday, these sixty titles were priced at just 60 pence each, and sold in their millions.

2000

Acquisition of Dorling Kindersley, the world's leading illustrated publisher.

Taken from concept to delivery in less than five months, sixty titles, made up of extracts from backlisted books, were priced at just 60 pence each, and they sold in their millions. This prompted publication of a further 120 titles. The series was an astounding commercial success, and played havoc with the UK bestseller lists.

Around this time, Penguin UK saw some bold restructuring of its publishing operations, overseen by a new chief executive. This was Anthony Forbes Watson, who had arrived from running a small but highly successful UK children's imprint, Ladybird Books (acquired by Pearson in 1972). The editorial department was revitalized by a new team led by Helen Fraser, who joined from Reed's trade books business. The benefits were quick to appear. Penguin won the UK's Publisher of the Year award for the first time in 1999, and revenues, due to a slew of big new authors, began climbing at a steady lick.

Then in the year 2000 came the acquisition of Dorling Kindersley (DK). Led since 1974 by a visionary graphic designer, Peter Kindersley, DK had revolutionized the art of laying out information with integrated photographs, graphics and text for a general readership. DK had had a severe setback over Christmas 1999, stocking a tie-in book of the *Star Wars: Episode I – The Phantom Menace* film in excessively large quantities. A financial crisis ensued, and Pearson bought the company three months later, merging it into Penguin.

O ur American roots
Penguin first set up shop in New York in July 1939. Plans to export books from the UK soon fell foul of the war. After Pearl Harbor, though, the armed forces' demand for paperbacks proved as big a boon in the US as in the UK. Some titles originated and published in the US sold in huge numbers, and Penguin Books Inc. was reputedly shipping a million books a month by the end of hostilities.

After the war, Penguin Books Inc. settled down to being a Baltimore-based distributor of exports from the UK. About half of these consisted of Penguin Classics, which were sold through college reps to campus bookshops. It was a lucrative enough business, but it was detached from the mainstream of US trade publishing, and remained so until 1975. That was the year Penguin's board, fearing the end of the old rights world might be nigh, took the plunge and purchased one of the most prestigious American trade houses, The Viking Press.

The Viking Press

In 1975, Penguin acquired The Viking Press, a top American hardback house.

On the Road

Jack Kerouac's post-war-defining novel was published in 1957 by The Viking Press. Based on his own road trips, *The New York Times* hailed it as 'the most beautifully executed, the clearest and most important utterance' of a generation.

The Viking Press had been a force in US publishing for ten years before Penguin was a twinkle in Allen Lane's eye, and by 1975 it had acquired a proud history of its own. It was set up in 1925 by two young men, Harold Guinzburg and George Oppenheim, who had walked away from jobs with the nascent firms of Simon & Schuster and Alfred A. Knopf. Like Allen Lane a decade later, they combined entrepreneurial flair with more than a touch of idealism. Their goal, they told the trade press, was 'to acclaim treasure when we find it, but to avoid calling brass gold...' And, like Penguin, they happened on a powerful trademark. The firm was going to call itself the Half Moon Press, until they discovered that the ship colophon it had commissioned was such a compelling drawing of a Viking longboat that a change of name was required.

Over the half century leading to 1975, Viking published a long list of the greatest American writers, from John Steinbeck and Saul Bellow to Jack Kerouac and Thomas Pynchon, and its roster of top British writers included Graham Greene, Iris Murdoch and Kingsley Amis. It also built a leading position in American juvenile publishing. Not the least of the many striking parallels between Viking and Penguin by 1975 was the depth and quality of the US firm's backlist. The merger of the two houses as Viking Penguin opened the way for a more concerted pursuit of the vertical publishing model. It brought Penguin a much higher US profile, and a shared office on Madison Avenue.

Bringing aboard Putnam

Peter Mayer always retained a strong affinity with the street-trading vigour of the US commercial market at its best. And in 1987 he pushed through the acquisition of New American Library. With its Signet and Mentor paperback imprints it gave the group a real presence in the US mass-market for the first time. It also owned the Plume imprint, with its mostly non-fiction trade paperback list. Assimilating NAL and Viking Penguin under one roof took up much of Peter's time over the next few years. When the time came for

1838

George Palmer Putnam established his first publishing house, Wiley & Putnam, in New York, which later became G. Putnam Broadway and then G. P. Putnam's Sons.

1996

Acquisition of Putnam Berkley Group, one of the oldest, largest and most prestigious names in US publishing.

his successor to be found, it was Peter who alerted his colleagues at Pearson to the potential availability for the job of another New Yorker. Michael Lynton, though only thirty-six, was living in Los Angeles and running Disney's Hollywood Pictures film studio when Pearson asked him to switch from blockbusters to books. Michael's appointment had scarcely been announced in the autumn of 1996 when there appeared a second announcement. One of Disney's conglomerate rivals in the world of films and theme parks was MCA Inc. Within Michael's first week at the office, Pearson agreed a deal with MCA to purchase its books division, which had been the target of bid rumours for many months. At a stroke, by acquiring the Putnam Berkley Group, Pearson now owned one of the oldest, largest and most prestigious names in US publishing.

The integrated US business was to be run by Phyllis Grann, who had been Putnam's chief executive since 1987. Phyllis was the archetype of a not uncommon phenomenon in publishing, the boss who began at the bottom. It was almost forty years since she had started as a secretary at Doubleday, and her steady rise to the top since then was a fair reflection of her driving personality.

The name itself acknowledged the scale and reputation of Putnam's operations. Its powerful list of bestselling authors was widely seen as the perfect complement to Penguin's backlist strengths and roughly doubled the size of Penguin's business in the US. Nor did their two histories provide any grounds for deference on either side. Putnam had a genealogy going back to 1838 (as noted on the spine of many of its books since April 2008). Its flagship hardback imprint, G. P. Putnam's Sons, had been a leading name in the US industry since 1872, when the founder's three sons marked his death by adding their assertive apostrophe.

Tracing its growth since then would be tantamount to plotting a history of the American publishing industry. Putnam had kept abreast of the growth of the commercial paperback market with a series of acquisitions that brought aboard several imprints, most notably Berkley Books (in 1965), Jove Books (in 1979) and Ace Books (in 1982). It had added to its hardback and trade paperback imprints by acquiring established names such as E. P. Dutton and Jeremy P. Tarcher. And it had also backed individual publishers keen to start up new imprints, like Riverhead Books, launched by

Susan Petersen Kennedy and three other editors in 1994. All these and others now joined Viking Penguin, NAL and the rest in Hudson Street – a teeming federation of imprints, each with its own lineage and lists, editors and marketing teams.

Pulling together

Half the challenge for Penguin Putnam was to ensure a happy and productive home environment for all its imprints. Phyllis Grann rose to the challenge by providing effective leadership wherever it was needed, and then letting the various cultures within the building thrive side by side. Judged by the number of published titles that made it on to *The New York Times* bestseller list, the new company was a resounding success: it outscored all of its rivals over the next few years.

Well connected

Good communication between the various departments and imprints is central to the commercial success at Penguin.

The other half of Penguin Putnam's challenge, though, was to find a way of realizing the potential value of a close rapport between Hudson Street and the rest of the Penguin Group. As different as the US and UK markets are, few in the late 1990s doubted the logic of seeking closer ties between colleagues on one side of the Atlantic and the other.

No executive rules or procedures could enforce a happy partnership. Editors pulled together or they didn't, depending on how much they liked and trusted each other as professional colleagues. That said, group arrangements could be conducive to closer relationships, given the right kind of leadership – meaning leaders with a full awareness of the opportunities on both sides of the Atlantic. Since 1996 Penguin's parent, Pearson, has had an American chief executive in Marjorie Scardino, which seemed a good start. And by the summer of 2002 Penguin had in John Makinson a chairman and chief executive who was already accustomed to dividing his time between London and New York.

John stepped into a role shaped originally by Peter Mayer and refined by Michael Lynton – but he made it clear from the outset that a closer integration of the group would involve far more than just a heavy travel schedule for the chairman. Increasingly, functions such as finance

Tarcher

Putnam acquired Jeremy P. Tarcher in 1991. The imprint has expanded from its original focus on health and philosophy to include serious non-fiction books of all types.

and technology would take on a global dimension. And in the same spirit, publishers and senior editors from both sides of the Atlantic – and from elsewhere too – would be encouraged to build closer informal ties with one another. It was an approach enthusiastically endorsed by the individuals running publishing operations in London and New York. Helen Fraser had assumed overall responsibility for all the many Penguin imprints in London since 1999, with Peter Field taking on the role of Penguin UK's CEO in 2006 (adding to his existing responsibilities as head of Pearson Australia Group). And in New York in 2001 Susan Petersen Kennedy had stepped up to become president, with David Shanks taking on CEO responsibilities for the business. There could be no disguising, of course, that the 1996 merger with Putnam had fundamentally changed the dynamics of the group. The sheer scale of the US operations and the size of their home marketplace put the whole business in a different light. But in a bold statement of intent in January 2003 the Penguin Putnam name in the US was dropped in favour of just plain Penguin. The group has gone forward as one entity – with many different dimensions, certainly, but as an unmistakably homogenous culture.

Riverhead

Since it was founded in 1994, Riverhead Books has been dedicated to publishing extraordinary ground-breaking, unique fiction and non-fiction writers.

3
Dignified, yet flippant
Our publishing in the US

When Penguin's founder, Allen Lane, was deliberating about which bird to use to symbolize the character of his book publishing company, he chose the penguin because it is a creature both dignified and flippant. Penguin US wholeheartedly embodies these defining characteristics today, publishing everything from entertaining *New York Times* bestselling fiction to brilliant Pulitzer prizewinning novels, and from practical non-fiction to vital narrative non-fiction about current events, politics and history.

When Chief Executive Officer, David Shanks and President, Susan Petersen Kennedy took the reins of the company in 2001 they rapidly developed a collegial environment and a personal management style that attracts and produces the brightest talent in the US publishing industry. The house is a mix of large and small imprints; some focus on a niche market and others publish into a broad range of subject areas. There is some overlap between imprints, which incites healthy competition and often generates fruitful dialogue about the best approach to publishing a particular book.

There are open, friendly relationships between imprints that at another company might regard one another as enemies. Penguin US employs a distinctive blend of entrepreneurial, aggressive, yet cautious and nimble people. It is guided by the belief that words on a page empower readers, that literature's greatest purpose is to broaden our understanding of ourselves and the world we live in, and that books can change the world by spreading ideas and influencing the cultural conversation. But books should also be fun, and Penguin places a premium on publishing titles that provide readers with an imaginative escape from their day-to-day grind.

Classic but contemporary

Today's company is a honeycomb of more than forty imprints. Brought together under one roof are venerable publishing houses founded long before the advent of the paperback, alongside imprints founded within the last decade that have quickly found their footing and are contributing to the group's list of literary award-winners and multi-million-copy bestsellers.

Of course these individual publishers and their imprint teams have different ways of working. But one characteristic is widely shared – the emphasis on 'repeat authors'. Penguin US strives to publish beloved authors year after year, and to bring those writers to readers in whatever format the reader prefers.

Modern legends

Penguin is the exclusive paperback publisher of Modern Classics' authors such as Saul Bellow, Arthur Miller and John Steinbeck.

Penguin the imprint, the namesake of the group, has a rich and varied history in the US as both a major commercial frontlist publisher and a renowned publisher of the classics. Penguin is the exclusive paperback publisher of Modern Classics' authors such as Saul Bellow, Arthur Miller and John Steinbeck.

The Penguin list continues to grow, to embrace new writers, and to keep in print the works of some of the world's most important authors. Readers' needs and tastes change, and the Penguin list has evolved over more than sixty years. Today, Penguin Classics comprise over 1,300 titles, making it the largest publisher of ancient and modern classic literature in the English-speaking world.

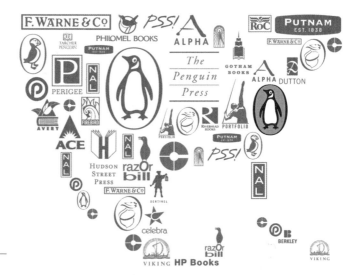

United States

Main office:
New York

Penguin Putnam merger:
1996

Authors include:
Geraldine Brooks, Harlan Coben, J. M. Coetzee, Patricia Cornwell, Junot Díaz, Ken Follett, Elizabeth Gilbert, Sue Grafton, Khaled Hosseini, Sue Monk Kidd, Greg Mortenson, Michael Pollan, Thomas Pynchon, Zadie Smith, Eckhart Tolle

CEO: David Shanks

Led by Penguin the imprint, Penguin US has broken new ground in recent years: trade paperback multi-million-copy bestsellers, which many in the industry thought unachievable. A report from Associated Press in April 2008 focused on the amazing feat of sales of more than thirteen million copies of just five of Penguin US's trade paperbacks in the space of a few months. All five – including Sue Monk Kidd's *The Secret Life of Bees* and Elizabeth Gilbert's *Eat, Pray, Love* – were by debut writers or little-known authors.

Following tradition, discovering trends
Berkley is the host to a creative cluster of imprints that includes New American Library, ACE (founded in 1953, the oldest continuously operating science-fiction publisher in the US) and Jove (founded in 1949). Today, the Berkley Group publishes over seven hundred titles a year in mass-market paperback, trade paperback and hardcover formats. Annually, more than a hundred of Berkley's books will reliably make the bestseller lists. Berkley is an undisputed leader in the mass-market sector with an uncanny ability to spot trends ahead of competitors and to sign up the best authors in the rising category.

The Little Engine That Could

This classic story teaches the value of optimism and hard work. Various large engines refuse to pull a train over a mountain, and only the small engine will try. It succeeds, while repeating the motto, 'I think I can'.

Traditional but edgy

Penguin in the US has a Young Readers Group that brings together fourteen imprints, all served by central marketing and sales departments. In at least two respects, the prominence of the division could be predicted by anyone knowing a little of the history of Viking children's books. It has a long lineage, which has left it with some superb backlists, full of classics such as S. E. Hinton's *The Outsiders* (the all-time bestselling young adult book ever published) and Robert McCloskey's *Make Way for Ducklings*. Dutton Children's Books is one of the oldest continually operating children's book publishers in the US, and their books include the *Winnie-the-Pooh* stories.

Beyond its rich tradition and lore, the Young Readers Group is also notable for a less predictable virtue: it is unafraid of experimenting with new writers whose work may end up expanding the boundaries of publishing for young people. Razorbill and Philomel are newer imprints and they publish books for young adults that stretch the limits of the imagination, as well as social convention.

Always looking forward

Many of Penguin US's forebears distinguished themselves with their entrepreneurial forward thinking. George Palmer Putnam was the first American publisher to set up shop in London in 1841 and the first to offer author royalties.

Madeline

Ludwig Bemelmans's children's book character, *Madeline*, first appeared in 1939. The books were adapted for TV and film and continue today, written by Bemelmans's grandson.

Nearly a century later Allen Lane democratized reading by popularizing the paperback. In 1988 Putnam Berkley became the first publisher to begin acquiring electronic display rights in order to publish works in an electronic format; in 1991 Putnam made a deal to publish eBook editions of William Gibson's first three novels; Penguin US was the first publisher to sell books directly to consumers on the internet; and a whole decade before Amazon released the Kindle, Penguin US began an eBooks program.

Ferdinand the Bull

The Story of Ferdinand (1936) by Munro Leaf, illustrated by Robert Lawson, tells the story of a bull who would rather smell flowers than fight in bullfights.

David Shanks followed in the footsteps of George Palmer Putnam when he came up with the idea of a brand new paperback format. He noted that while trade paperbacks were soaring in popularity, the mass-market was looking a bit soft. And so he proposed the premium paperback, priced at $9.99 rather than $7.99. The premium features larger type and is designed for a more luxurious reading experience than with a traditional mass-market book. The new format was a hit with baby boomers, and is responsible for a distinct revival of mass-market sales across the industry.

In this same tradition of entrepreneurial spirit, Shanks and Kennedy have brought a number of new imprints to the Penguin Group.

Read for the Record with Corduroy

Over 425,000 American children took part in Jumpstart's Read for the Record campaign in 2008. The event broke the world record for the largest shared-reading experience, and raised almost $2 million for early education programmes.

The Very Hungry Caterpillar

Eric Carle's delightful story is one of the bestselling books of all time, charming millions of young readers since its publication in 1969.

Khaled Hosseini

Hosseini was born in Afghanistan, and is now an American citizen. His 2003 debut novel, *The Kite Runner*, has sold over 6.75 million copies in the US. His second novel, *A Thousand Splendid Suns*, has sold more than 3 million copies in the US to date.

Kennedy herself founded Riverhead more than a decade ago and from the very first season published an inspired array of bestselling and award-winning authors, including James McBride, Thich Nhat Hanh, the Dalai Lama, Nick Hornby, Anne Lamott, Junot Díaz, who won the Pulitzer Prize for his novel *The Brief Wondrous Life of Oscar Wao*, and Khaled Hosseini, author of *The Kite Runner* and *A Thousand Splendid Suns*.

Susan Petersen Kennedy believes that great publishing usually involves a small group of people working together with intensity and total dedication to their writers and readers. The need for a close relationship with every author sets a natural limit to each group's size. This belief was part of the inspiration for founding Gotham, Portfolio and The Penguin Press. These new imprints are flourishing; in its second year of business, more than a third of the books published by The Penguin Press hit *The New York Times* bestseller list.

The Penguin way

Constant communication between the various departments and imprints is a hallmark of Penguin US culture. Collegiality is the watchword. It is exemplified in the two breakfast meetings – one for hardbacks, the other for paperbacks – at which all of the teams come together each week to review current progress. Around the table on these occasions are not just the editors and publishers with their marketing and PR teams, but representatives of the support functions as well – including members of production and inventory control. Critically, they are also attended by all the senior staff of the respective sales departments. The working relationship between the editorial and sales teams at Penguin US is probably the best in the industry and is often cited as one of its key strengths.

The existence of separate sales forces for hardback and paperback books is now highly unusual. But it remains a firm belief within the company that each market has a fundamentally different dynamic, best served by a distinct approach. The hardback force is in constant dialogue with editors, as well as with retail accounts. This communication is critical to successfully positioning new authors within the market and making smart decisions about how and when to publish a particular book.

Penguin Classics Deluxe Editions
Each luxury volume features French
flaps, special paper and rough-cut
edges, as well as the literary and
educational extras for which the
Penguin Classics are known.

Its twenty or so salespeople are avid readers of the new lists each year, and they work closely with marketing and publicity in each imprint to find the broadest audience for each book published. This is not an easy task, given that they are invariably asked to bring unknown authors to the marketplace.

Their remarkable success comes in part from relentless attention to retailers' buying patterns, combined with hard-hitting campaigns to reinforce the success of titles that have begun to show signs of attracting buzz. Because it is separate, the paperback sales force will bring a fresh set of eyes to the same books when they reappear. They will carefully study the existing sales pattern and may even bring a new sense of the readership for a particular book. The paperback sales force also tends to the backlist and creates promotions that will keep backlist books top of mind and front of store.

There is no space here to do justice to the professionalism of each team at Penguin US, from the editors to the designers, and from the marketers to production, operations and transportation. They are motivated and united by the belief that their work brings high-quality entertainment, soul-satisfying enlightenment, and a greater understanding of the world, past and present, to readers everywhere.

What came before?
Our US history

George Palmer Putnam
(1814 – 72)

1830s

In the 1830s, George Palmer Putnam and John Wiley established and ran the publishing house of Wiley & Putnam in New York City. Together they published the likes of Herman Melville, Edgar Allan Poe, Nathaniel Hawthorne, Charles Dickens and Elizabeth Barrett Browning.

1840s

In 1841 Putnam went to London and became the first American ever to set up a branch office there. Almost a hundred years later, in 1939, Allen Lane would travel the opposite way across the Atlantic to set up an American branch of Penguin in New York. Putnam soon dissolved his partnership with Wiley and renamed the company G. Putnam Broadway. He then went on to publish Washington Irving, William Cullen Bryant and James Fenimore Cooper. Putnam was a Renaissance man. In addition to his prominence in the book world, he founded *Putnam's Monthly magazine* (an antecedent to today's *Atlantic Monthly*) with Frederick Law Olmsted, who later designed Central Park and dozens of other North American landmark parks. Putnam was a founder of the Metropolitan Museum of Art, and he was its first superintendent.

He was active in the Publishers Association, an advocate of the creation of international copyright law, and he is believed to have been the first publisher to offer royalties to authors.

1850s

Dutton is yet another storied imprint within Penguin US. Edward Payson Dutton *(1831 – 1923)*, its founder, is buried at Trinity Cemetery in Washington Heights (only a few miles from the Hudson Street offices). He started a bookselling company in Boston in 1852. Twelve years later he opened a New York office and began publishing books focused on religion. The company went on to publish books by John Irving (*The World According to Garp*), Peter Matthiessen and Jorge Luis Borges. A century and a half after Dutton sold its first book, the publishing house has maintained its ability to get great books into the hands of many readers. In 2006 and 2007 one in every four books published by Dutton hit *The New York Times* bestseller lists.

DUTTON

1880s

Over the years, numerous public figures would contribute to Putnam in various ways. In the 1880s

Theodore Roosevelt was a special partner to G.P. Putnam's Sons. He wrote several works published by Putnam, including *Naval War of 1812* and *The Winning of the West.*

1900s

On into the twentieth century, Putnam continued to blaze a controversial literary path, publishing Norman Mailer's *Deer Park* and Vladimir Nabokov's *Lolita*. Both books were banned in some countries and elicited firestorms of public debate about censorship. Today, the imprint continues to dominate *The New York Times* bestseller lists: roughly half of the books Putnam publishes land on the *Times* lists, which is the gold standard of achievement in the US market.

1920s

Viking was originally founded in 1925 and joined with Penguin fifty years later. Its founders Harold Guinzburg and George Oppenheim (who'd left their respective positions at Simon & Schuster and Alfred A. Knopf) were planning to call the company Half Moon Press. But when the illustrator they'd commissioned to design a logo, Rockwell Kent, delivered to them a drawing of a Viking longboat, they changed their minds. They adopted the image as the Viking logo to represent exploration and enterprise.

In one of his first forays into book publishing, George Palmer Putnam's grandson and namesake, George P. Putnam *(1887 – 1950)*, published Charles Lindbergh's autobiography *We*. In 1928, as a result, a wealthy American woman living in London asked Putnam to find a woman who would undertake the first ever flight across the Atlantic Ocean. He came up with the then unknown Amelia Earhart. After she completed the flight successfully, Putnam published two books about her flying adventures and organized Earhart's public engagements and speaking tour across

the US, in what was perhaps the first book tour. Putnam went above and beyond with Earhart, arranging for endorsement contracts with a luggage manufacturer and a line of ladies' sportswear, and eventually marrying her! It seems that book publishing always has been an intimate business.

1950s

American literary legends such as Jack Kerouac, Saul Bellow and Arthur Miller are part of Viking's legacy, which also includes a host of bestselling and prize-winning contemporary authors. Literary history is tangible at Viking. The current director of non-fiction at Viking works at the desk of Pascal Covici, who edited John Steinbeck's *East of Eden*. And the marketing director works at the desk that was Malcolm Cowley's when he was an editorial consultant to Viking and pushed for Jack Kerouac's *On the Road* to be published.

Amelia Earhart
(1897 – 1939)

RACHEL CARSON
Under the Sea-Wind

The Penguin Book of English Verse

JACK KEROUAC
On the Road
With an Introduction by ANN CHARTERS

JOHN STEINBECK
Of Mice and Men

SAUL BELLOW
Humboldt's Gift

WALLACE STEGNER AND
PAGE STEGNER
American Places

GUSTAVE FLAUBERT
Madame Bovary

KARL MARX AND
FRIEDRICH ENGELS
The Communist Manifesto

REBECCA WEST
Black Lamb and Grey Falcon
A Journey Through Yugoslavia

HOMER
The Odyssey
Translated by ROBERT FAGLES

KNUT HAMSUN
Growth of the Soil

HOMER
The Iliad

JORGE LUIS BORGES
Brodie's Report

JANE AUSTEN
Emma

RYŪNOSUKE AKUTAGAWA
Rashōmon and Seventeen Other Stories

CAO XUEQIN AND GAO E
The Story of the Stone
Volume IV

4

Something for everyone

Our publishing in the UK

E ver since its successful reorganization in 1997, Penguin UK has divided its adult publishing into two distinct divisions. The larger of these is Penguin General, and its approach to publishing goes beyond the traditional book business model in some intriguing ways. It aims to select and build adult fiction and non-fiction brands across a whole range of media, retail and digital platforms. Above all, though, it is defined by its diversity. It wants to publish the very best of every category of book for all parts of the market – with a strong emphasis on bestsellers as the clearest sign of a healthy and vibrant publishing operation.

By far the most fertile ground for bestsellers in the UK is the commercial fiction sector of the market. This was a concern to Penguin back in the mid 1990s, when it was a distant also-ran in this field and saw that it was poorly placed to respond to the rapid growth that clearly lay ahead. Remedying Penguin's perceived vulnerability was the challenge handed to Helen Fraser when she joined the business as Penguin General's managing director at the start of 1997.

To celebrate the 100th anniversary of Ian Fleming's birth, all 14 Bond books were re-issued with new covers. The artwork was created by painter Michael Gillette.

elen resolved to turn the division's Michael Joseph imprint into a powerhouse of commercial publishing – and with authors such as Marian Keyes, Jane Green and Lesley Pearse, Michael Joseph is now a clear leader in women's fiction.

In that other key fiction category, the crime and thriller genre, Penguin was less adrift a decade ago but was nowhere near the kind of ascendancy it enjoyed in the 1950s. Again, huge progress has been made in recent years, with US authors such as Tom Clancy and Clive Cussler joining long-established British writers like P. D. James and Dick Francis. There is much further to go if Michael Joseph's resurgence in crime is to parallel what has been achieved in women's fiction. But don't bet against it. And, meanwhile, another list has been created in roughly the same area labelled Boy's Fiction which includes, among other gems, the James Bond portfolio.

Penguin's leading share of the popular non-fiction hardback market is another reflection of Michael Joseph's resurgence. Its editors are widely admired for the professionalism of their publishing across a dauntingly eclectic range of subjects, from celebrity autobiographies and sports books to TV tie-ins and the (hugely popular) thoughts of Jeremy Clarkson – plus, of course, cookery. A new name emerged from the kitchen in 1998 and Penguin took him on for his first book, *The Naked Chef*. Some eight titles later, and with millions of books sold in both hardback and paperback, Jamie Oliver has become a publishing phenomenon in the UK market and is well on his way to becoming a globally recognized brand name.

Above all, good writing

Other imprints within Penguin General tend to be aimed at what might be considered more traditional Penguin targets. The first of these is a broad category of books – mostly, but by no means exclusively, fiction – distinguished by good writing, a strong narrative and a subject matter that will reliably engage the kind of people who, in their millions, increasingly like to belong to reading groups. This is very much the franchise of the Viking imprint in London. Viking publishes about forty titles a year, with a small number of paperback originals, and its books need to sell – either as hardbacks or as Penguin paperbacks – everywhere from the most recherché bookshop to the supermarket shelves.

'Top Five' books

One of Nick Hornby's best-known novels, *High Fidelity*, has been adapted into a film and a Broadway musical. Other titles published by Penguin include *Fever Pitch, How to be Good, A Long Way Down* and *Slam*, his first book aimed at teenagers.

Global bestseller

The Catcher in the Rye has sold over 65 million copies worldwide.

Viking's list includes novelists such as Nick Hornby and Kim Edwards, author of the global bestseller *The Memory Keeper's Daughter*. A second imprint, and a recent addition in this area, is Fig Tree, which is already enjoying more bestsellers in its early days than any newish imprint has a right to expect.

Meanwhile, of course, Penguin continues to cherish the kind of publishing that generations of past editors held dear – working with the most distinguished contemporary writers of literary fiction and serious non-fiction, especially history, biography and current affairs. Once again, Viking has a significant presence here as the publisher of authors such as William Trevor, Colm Tóibín, Antony Beevor and Claire Tomalin.

Another key imprint in this sector is Hamish Hamilton. Acquired for the group by Peter Mayer in the 1980s, 'Hamish' has a famous history stretching back to 1931 and can boast a backlist that includes names like Salinger, Capote, Camus and Sebald. Today, Hamish takes good care of its legacy – J. D. Salinger's *The Catcher in the Rye* is still one of Penguin UK's top ten bestselling titles, year after year – while nurturing a small group of writers whose books it can envisage remaining on the backlist for generations to come. It only publishes around twenty titles a year, half fiction and half non-fiction, and many of those will do well if they sell 10,000 copies. But with authors such as Jonathan Safran Foer, Mohsin Hamid, Ali Smith and Alain de Botton, there is always the possibility that Hamish will come up with another huge seller – as it did in 2000 with Zadie Smith's *White Teeth*, which in various editions has now sold over a million copies.

Those famous names

All of the UK imprints mentioned so far belong to the Penguin General division. However, the Penguin Press division, which has been twinned with it since 1997, is home to most of Penguin UK's serious non-fiction publishing, plus today's extended family of Penguin Classics. This famous name sits beside another, Allen Lane, whose imprint has carved out a leading position in current affairs, history and popular science publishing in the UK.

United Kingdom

Main office:
London

Established:
1935

Authors include:
Antony Beevor, Alain de
Botton, Jeremy Clarkson,
Eoin Colfer, Clive Cussler,
Niall Ferguson, Malcolm
Gladwell, Jane Green,
Mohsin Hamid, Zoë Heller,
Charlie Higson, Nick
Hornby, Marian Keyes,
Marina Lewycka, Jamie
Oliver, Meg Rosoff, Zadie
Smith, Claire Tomalin

CEO: Peter Field

Brains and words

Penguin author Malcolm Gladwell has been named 'the most influential thinker for the iPod generation' by UK newspaper *The Observer*.

Where Penguin General will prosper if its imprints hold a mirror to the marketplace, those imprints under Penguin Press must offer books that open windows for the reader into new worlds, providing unfamiliar perspectives and fresh insights.

Allen Lane's current pre-eminence dates back to the mid 1990s, with the arrival of a string of gifted new editors who quickly attracted a dazzling array of widely admired and bestselling authors. Among the historians were Ian Kershaw (Hitler's biographer) and Niall Ferguson (chronicler of wars and empires), while the scientists included Steven Pinker (on brains and language) and Jared Diamond (on everything else). More recently, Allen Lane has enjoyed equal success in that harder-to-categorize field of ideas-driven non-fiction associated with psychology, economics, business and society – books such as Nassim Nicholas Taleb's *The Black Swan* and Malcolm Gladwell's *Outliers*.

'Red' the Classics yet?

The Red Classics series, launched in 2006, is aimed at winning first-time readers, with its range of 1930s poster-style jackets.

The Penguin Classics have enjoyed something of a rebirth in the past few years. With a backlist of over 1,300 titles – around 900 of them comprising the Black Classics, with their high quota of translated works, and the rest made up of the Modern Classics, with their jackets bordered in silver – the series presents a constant publishing challenge. This is, after all, probably the largest collection of its kind in all of world literature, so no set of revisions will ever finish the job. Editors must keep up a stream of ideas to refresh the series for each new generation. Today, the work goes on as creatively as ever. Scholarly translations are being given new introductions by leading writers such as Martin Amis, Peter Ackroyd and Philip Pullman. And a series of Red Classics was launched in 2006, aimed at winning over first-time readers to the great classic stories. Shorn of all notes and appendixes, these are packaged like original fiction, with covers to match.

I n 2005 another classics paperback series was launched, christened *Great Ideas*. Its premise was that august authors such as Freud or Darwin should not be seen as producing 'all-or-nothing' texts, to be revered in the catalogue but scarcely read. Could not compelling extracts from their work be used to entice new readers, with at least the gist of the full original? *Great Ideas* set out to do just this, putting a hundred pages or so of each author in a slim paperback with an arresting cover. A resounding success, the first forty titles sold over two million copies.

Rearing new readers

Classics have always been a mainstay of one other sector too – children's books. But there is much more to successful publishing in this sector than brilliant repackaging of the great stories of the past, essential as this will nevertheless be. (Children, as every publisher forgets at their peril, can be among the most conservative of all readers.) There is also a constant call for exciting new work, which must be calibrated very precisely to whichever age group is being targeted. Penguin enjoys a leading position in the UK market on the strength of five children's imprints – Puffin, DK Children's, BBC Children's Books, Frederick Warne and Ladybird. The largest of these is Puffin.

Puffin Classics

Puffin's mission is to publish the best quality books for children. As with the early Penguins, the first Puffins, published in 1940, were pioneers of their genre.

L aunched in 1940, Puffin's mission from the start was to publish the best possible books for children as high-quality paperbacks. As with the first Penguins, which had appeared just five years earlier, the first Puffins were pioneers of their genre. Today, Puffin publishes in hardback as well as paperback, but the original objective is unchanged. It has built a list of great books, encompassing both the iconic titles loved for generations and the work of exciting contemporary authors, many of whose names are already well on their way to being icons of the future.

Those titles already assured of lasting fame span all age groups. There are picture books for the youngest readers, which include Eric Carle's *The Very Hungry Caterpillar* (one of Puffin's most successful titles), Raymond Briggs's *The Snowman* and Janet and Allan Ahlberg's *Each Peach Pear Plum*.

Great Ideas

Some books have changed the world, transforming the way we see ourselves, and each other. The Great Ideas series introduced the writing of great thinkers, pioneers, radicals and visionaries to new readers.

John Ruskin's *On Art and Life* sold just a couple of hundred copies a year until it was transformed into a pocket-sized read that sold 30,000 copies in six months.

Great Ideas Red
2006

Great Ideas Green
2008

Great Ideas Blue
2007

The Snowman

Raymond Briggs's *The Snowman* is
one of the UK's best-loved stories,
featuring largely in most families'
Christmas Day celebrations.

'The world's favourite storyteller'

From the publication of *James and the Giant Peach* in 1961 to his death in 1990, Roald Dahl became the bestselling children's author in the world, and his tales are still enjoyed by millions of children today.

Contemporary fiction for children

Puffin's Artemis Fowl and Young Bond series are constants on children's favourites lists. Young Bond is a series of novels by Charlie Higson about James Bond as a teenager at Eton in the 1930s.

There are modern classics, including Richard Adams's *Watership Down*, and then there is Roald Dahl – whose status as the Penguin Group's single biggest-selling author in any genre perhaps entitles him to that usually inflated sobriquet of the 'world's favourite storyteller'.

Given its reputation, Puffin has no difficulty in attracting its share of the most talented current writers for children. The challenge for its editors, now more than ever, is to help those writers attract today's savvy young readers in a busy and furiously competitive retail market. Puffin approaches every new title knowing it must deliver the whole package of design and artwork, plus marketing and online campaigns, in addition to its traditional skills of editing.

The most successful authors are encouraged to develop as brands in themselves, and long-term strategies are devised to help them grow their profiles in the marketplace with each successive title they produce. This is the careful support work that for many Puffin authors has helped to secure a strong following from readers aged between nine and twelve, who traditionally comprise the largest sector of the children's market. Contemporary 'branded' writers include Eoin Colfer with his Artemis Fowl books, and Charlie Higson with his Young Bond series.

This same publishing philosophy underpins Puffin's work for teenage readers, and today's list includes award-winning authors such as Melvin Burgess (*Junk* is a modern-classic bestseller) and Meg Rosoff. Marketing to teen readers can take real inventiveness, and Puffin is constantly looking for ways to beat the competition. It recently launched the first website to be run by teenagers for teenagers – spinebreakers.co.uk – and it has repackaged its classics list with great success, asking major contemporary authors to write introductions to their favourite classics. This combination of the traditional and the contemporary is a nice encapsulation of what Puffin is all about, as it prepares for its seventieth birthday in 2010.

Peter Rabbit is the lead character in a series of books by Beatrix Potter. He first appeared in print in 1902 and as a soft toy in 1903, making him the oldest licensed character in the world.

Beatrix Potter © Frederick Warne & Co., 2008.

TM

TM

Flower Fairies

Cicely Mary Barker published her first *Flower Fairies* story in 1923, creating seven more volumes over the next 30 years.

Flower Fairies © The Estate of Cicely Mary Barker, 2008.

TM

In the Night Garden

BBC Children's Books has sold over 4.6 million copies of the popular children's series books charting the adventures of Upsy Daisy, Makka Pakka and Igglepiggle.

In the Night Garden TM & © Ragdoll Worldwide Ltd.

Beyond the world of print

Finally, there is one other team within the Penguin UK company for whom the concept of brand marketing and merchandising lies at the centre of everything. This is the Brands and Licensing division, built up over the years on the foundation laid by the acquisition in the 1970s of Frederick Warne, with all its rights to Peter Rabbit.

Peter Rabbit's creator, Beatrix Potter, knew all about the potential value of a fictional character, once brought alive in the imagination of millions of readers. Back in 1903, she used her own illustrations to design first a prototype 'doll' of Peter Rabbit, and then a tea set featuring all the characters (even the rake-toting Mr McGregor) from the little storybooks she had created. From there she embarked on what she called her 'little side-shows', selling a range of spin-off products branded with Peter Rabbit – launching the start of his career in merchandising.

Today, it is far from a 'little side-show' for Penguin. The World of Beatrix Potter has hundreds of licensees worldwide. And Peter Rabbit has been joined in the division by a cast of other characters, from *Topsy and Tim* to the *Flower Fairies* and *Dr Who*. They have been collected via the acquisition of the Ladybird imprint and the establishment of BBC Children's Books, a joint venture with the BBC which is aimed at exploiting the branded content of programmes for

Topsy and Tim

The twins' stories were first
published in 1960, and were
relaunched in 2003. The books
have sold more than 21 million
copies worldwide.

© Jean and Gareth Adamson, MCMXCV.

TM

TM

both toddlers (such as *In the Night Garden*) and young
adults, or indeed their parents (such as *Top Gear*).
Part of what keeps it so lively is the extraordinary scope
for powerful brands to travel the world. They can be
popular not just in English-speaking countries, but in
foreign-language markets too.

Spot, the lovable dog created by Eric Hill and first
published in 1980, enjoys one of his strongest
followings in the Netherlands, where he goes by
the name of Dribbel (not, perhaps, a contender
for English-speaking markets).

Repositioning familiar characters to suit them to new
markets is one of the main challenges facing the Brands and
Licensing team, and some adjustments go beyond a simple
name change. It seems appropriate that *Peter Rabbit*, who
started it all, should have become the first licensed property
to feature in a comprehensive ethical and environmental
programme, *Peter Rabbit, Naturally Better*.

Where's Spot?

First published in 1980, Eric Hill's
Spot series has been incredibly
successful with translations into
over 60 languages.

Spot © Eric Hill/Salspot, 2008.

5

Here, there and everywhere

Dorling Kindersley and travel publishing

There are international dimensions to the group's operations in both the US and the UK, but it was legitimate in the previous sections to identify them strongly with their home markets. Dorling Kindersley (DK) is a different matter entirely. DK's international dimensions are the essence of its business. Its largest single sales market is the US. Its international licensing and publishing operation is based in London, alongside Penguin UK's other divisions, at 80 Strand. (Before that, DK was based in London's Covent Garden, expanding over the years into a complex rabbit warren of small offices.) DK's in-house creative work is split between London and New Delhi, with smaller teams of editors and designers based in the US, Australia, Germany and Canada. And its basic business model is all about creating books that can be licensed for parallel sales in any number of local language markets. If ever there was a truly global business, this is it.

DK

was founded by Christopher Dorling and Peter Kindersley in the 1970s with a fund of only £10,000. A fire at the Dutch reproduction house where DK's first three books had been sent threatened to bring the venture to a premature end, but the small team managed to defy the odds and to deliver all three books within their deadlines. Both founders are now retired from the business, with Kindersley running a successful organic farm inspired by one of his own books from the 1970s, *The Complete Book of Self-Sufficiency*, which was one of the first guides to living off the land.

DK's business model is based on the concept of combining photography, graphics and type in highly distinctive ways. At first, this was done to revolutionize the design of dense, information-heavy copy (which it duly accomplished), but it was quickly appreciated that it could also be used to transform the art of packaging books. The typical DK format would allow the text to be extracted, modified and reinserted at minimal cost, so that different language versions of one title could be produced without redesigning the original. The full potential of this was unveiled in style in 1991, when DK co-produced a book with the UN Conference on Environmental Development, *Save the Earth*, and printed it in seventeen different languages for simultaneous publication across the world.

Since then, DK has perfected the business of researching and creating a new book for a clearly identified market niche, locating 'co-edition partners' to provide local-language translations of the master text, printing the various editions with a fierce eye on costs, and then licensing them out to those partners for sale in their discrete markets. Of course, these same partners could invariably find locally produced books that would be far cheaper – so the onus is always on DK to come up with work of a conspicuously superior quality. It achieves this by devoting obsessive attention to the quality of its production methods and to the originality of its designs. DK's creative teams assemble photographs, artwork and copy into 'packages' in ways that have been endlessly refined over many years with the help of a global network of artists, photographers and consultants.

Make the Most of Your Time on Earth

Featuring 1,000 of the best travel experiences, this book offers inspiration to both the seasoned traveller and the armchair dreamer.

Faster than technology

Published within weeks of the iPhone launch in the US, *The Rough Guide to the iPhone* was ready to hit UK before the device even reached the shelves.

Did you know?

A Rough Guide is purchased somewhere in the world every ten seconds.

Cleaner, greener books

DK's Made with Care titles are made using the most ethical and environmental processes possible, and for every book sold through Amazon DK donates a book to the charity Book Aid International.

The result is a business that leads the world in the design of illustrated books, for both adults and children, and that never runs short of prospective partners for whatever blockbuster title it is planning next.

Past and present titles have covered an impressive range of subjects. All might broadly be categorized as 'reference' works, summarizing encyclopaedic quantities of facts in accessible and entertaining ways. Health and well-being, science and nature, sports and hobbies, food and drink – all have been presented in the unique DK format. Many of the titles have been devised in partnership with the leading authority on the topic at hand. For example, DK has worked closely with the Royal Horticultural Society since 1989, and the resulting series of publications has transformed the world of gardening books. Another important partner has come from within the Pearson group: DK has joined forces with Pearson Education to bring its design values to bear on school materials. This is one aspect of a children's list at DK that also includes preschool books, activity books for five to eight year olds and – above all, of course – the celebrated Eyewitness series, which actually began life as a joint venture with the French publisher Gallimard, and has now grown to become the biggest-selling non-fiction series in publishing history.

No summary of DK's business would be complete without reference to two other features of its work. The first is the leadership it has shown on green issues since its very early days. It has led the way on innovations designed to make publishing as friendly as possible to the environment. Its Made with Care series of books, for example, are printed with vegetable ink on FSC (Forest Stewardship Council) paper, and have dispensed altogether with the need for dust jackets.

The second is the way in which DK has been naturally positioned at the forefront of the revolution in publishing technology. Around 1,000 of its non-travel books were available as eBooks by the end of 2008. And DK is now composing all of its book packages with software that will allow them to be stored in a massive digital database. It will be able to tap this for online publishing to screens of any size, down to the smallest mobile phone.

From apples...

...to zebras

Dorling Kindersley

If you want to know about it, there's a DK book that tells you about it. Just about every subject has been dissected, analysed and explained in simple text and illustrated with beautiful graphics.

DK Travel Awards

Guardian/Observer Award
DK Eyewitness Travel won best
guidebook series in 2004 and 2005.

Wanderlust Award DK Eyewitness
Travel won silver for best guidebook
series four years in a row, from 2003
to 2006, and bronze in 2007.

TravelMole Award traveldk.com
won best holiday/travel extras for
2007 and 2008.

Travolution Awards traveldk.com
won best use of technology in 2008.

T

ravel publishing
The DK approach to design was surely destined from the start to transform the art of travel guides, adding 3-D maps and floor plans where other publishers had dense paragraphs of italics. Its Eyewitness Travel series has grown since 1993 to become the biggest series of its kind in the world, greatly assisted by the co-edition model which allows new titles to appear in many different languages at once – more than thirty of them, in fact, for the most popular titles. In one of those slightly silly but nonetheless arresting facts that statistics can produce, we know DK now sells a travel guide somewhere in the world every four seconds. The series covers a hundred destinations around the globe and has spurred spin-off ideas like the DK Eyewitness Top 10 Travel Guides, which provide lists of every conceivable kind for each location – even the 'Top 10 Things to Avoid'.

As a group, though, Penguin has been twice blessed with its expansion into travel publishing. Some years prior to its acquisition of DK, the group had already begun a long and rewarding tie-up with the creators of the one series original enough to hold its own against DK – the Rough Guide series.

DK Eyewitness Top 10s

The DK Eyewitness Top 10 Travel Guides provide travel lists of every kind, including the 'Top 10 Things to Avoid'.

More than a decade before the first DK Eyewitness guides were published, *The Rough Guide to Greece* launched what has long since become one of the most familiar publishing brands around the world, selling more than thirty million books to date. One of the coolest, too – its witty and no-nonsense style has always marked it as something of a one-off, true to its humble beginnings in a London basement flat. It has built up a fiercely loyal readership over many years, allowing today's publishing team to move beyond travel into guides to metaphysical places such as world music and the mysteries of climate change. Indeed, *The Rough Guide to the Internet* is its bestselling book to date, with over three million copies sold worldwide.

Both imprints have been gearing up fast to keep abreast of rising demand for digital directions. Rough Guides, the first guidebook publisher to go online, is also making its content available to mobiles, with over seven million Motorola and Samsung phones in the UK and Europe now preloaded with Rough Guide information. Not to be outdone, Eyewitness Travel has pulled off a spectacular journey of its own: from having no website at all in 2006 to now having one of the most original. Visitors to traveldk.com can assemble their own tailored travel guides. And, for those who want it, DK will arrange to have your personally tailored guide printed as a glossy booklet.

The Rough Guide to Greece

1982's *Rough Guide to Greece* was conceived by Mark Ellingham, who was dissatisfied with existing guidebooks being 'cost-obsessed student guides or heavyweight cultural tomes'.

Pirates and ne'er-do-wells

The Rough Guide name has been much pirated over the years. The Church of England even produced a bootleg *Rough Guide to Marriage*.

6
Where in the world?
Our international publishing

Assemble a group of employees in any part of the group and ask them to list the reasons why they think Penguin is different – and you will almost certainly discover that a big part of the answer can be found on the back of the title page of every book. Who could ever work for Penguin, after all, without running their eye from time to time down that alluring list of addresses? Hudson Street and 80 Strand are just for starters. What exotic places might not be visited one day, such as Panchsheel Park or Eglinton Avenue? Albany, Camberwell or Rosebank?

The world of publishing is still some way short of being truly global, if by that we mean one integrated marketplace. And so long as separate copyright territories exist, there will be authors, agents and publishers who understandably believe their best interests may lie with a territorial approach to each of them. The trend towards local bestsellers and adaptations might even appear to contradict globalization, making the need for local relevance and appeal as much of a priority as ever.

B ut if the day does come when a single edition can be sold globally, Penguin's unique status on the international stage is surely going to be the one of the most striking features of the group. Indeed, in most of the ways that matter, Penguin already operates as a global company. It certainly does so effectively enough to be able to offer those authors and agents a sound reason for selling world rights to the one publisher that can really make them work.

What underpins this unique status? There are several answers. The group encompasses local publishing operations in more countries than any competitor. (And in many cases Penguin has had a presence in those markets for longer too. For example, while Penguin India was celebrating its twentieth anniversary in 2007, its peers were just setting up shop there.) The group embraces all of its geographically scattered activities within one culture, in ways that others can only theorize about. It coordinates its rights-selling activities in a more centralized fashion from New York and London than do any of its rivals. It runs by far the largest and most coordinated export-sales operation in the industry. And in DK it owns the pioneer, and still the most successful exponent, of co-edition global licensing.

Local publishing around the world

The US offshoot of Penguin operated for many years as little more than a distributor of UK books. But in Australia and New Zealand, India, South Africa and Canada it was a very different story. Once a warehouse and sales force had been established, a domestic publishing operation quickly took root.

T oday, all five companies have robust business models built around imports, local lists and agency contracts for the distribution of other UK and US houses' books. As international publishers they have to contend with plenty of problems. Penguin South Africa, for example, always has the exchange rate of the rand to worry about. Penguin Canada has to grapple with the challenges of dealing with one major retail channel that controls over 50 percent of the Canadian market. Penguin Australia has to ponder the impact of cheap imports and remainders if Australia were ever to scrap its own copyright territoriality.

20 years in India

Founded in 1987, Penguin India is Asia's largest English-language trade publisher.

YEARS OF PUBLISHING IN INDIA

Penguin India

Titles published in 1987:

7

Titles published in 2008:

204

Prize winning writers

Penguin India's authors have won virtually every major literary prize, including: the Nobel Prize, Magsaysay Award, Jnanpith Award, Man Booker Prize, Sahitya Akademi Award and the Commonwealth Writers' Prize.

Local publishing

Penguin encompasses local
publishing operations in more
countries than any competitor.

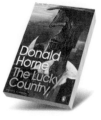

But through a resourceful use of the brand and the quality of
their editors, they have all won themselves leading positions
in their home markets – one indication of which is the fact
that in 2008 Australia, Canada and South Africa each won
Publisher of the Year awards in their respective markets.

Local publishing accounts for about 10 percent of
South Africa's revenues, 20 percent of Canada's,
50 percent of Australia's and 60 percent of India's.
They produce regular bestsellers –
though few make quite such a brilliant score
as Australian cricket captain Steve Waugh's
autobiography, which has sold over 200,000
copies in hardback since its publication in
2005. They create bestselling series, such as
Extraordinary Canadians, a collection of twenty eminent
biographies launched in the spring of 2008. And they have
begun in one case to publish non-English writers: Penguin
India, still a joint venture with the Kolkata-based *ABP*
newspaper and magazines group, publishes in Hindi,
Marathi and Urdu. Penguin India could also lay claim –
with authors such as Vikram Seth, William Dalrymple and
Amitav Ghosh – to being Asia's largest English-language
trade-book publisher by a considerable distance.

Street selling

Penguin India used a traditional sales technique for a recent book by blogger Meenakshi Reddy Madhavan. Copies were sold at traffic lights across the country.

This kind of dominance was reflected in 2008 in Penguin India's clean sweep of the Crossword Awards, India's most prestigious book awards.

What makes the group's geographical spread so extraordinary, though, is not just its diversity but the success with which all the Penguin companies now work together. This is only partly a result of the revolution in communications over the past twenty years. It is also the fruit of a group management initiative, diligently pursued. Everyone has a keener appreciation of the fact that all are working to the same corporate end. Sales people and business managers alike now travel much more extensively (though not unnecessarily, given the strength of green sentiments across the group). Above all, there is an unprecedented level of dialogue among publishers and editors. Corporate events, so often a half-hearted affair in other industries, have helped bring them together. Probably the most notable event of its kind is the annual Venice meeting, bringing together twenty or so of the group's leading publishers. Admission is strictly limited to those with direct responsibility for the acquiring and publishing of books: i.e. no suits. Its name derives from the location of the first meeting in 2001. But when it comes to building trust and mutual respect among editors, nothing is more important to the group than the working relationship between the sister companies on the two sides of the Atlantic.

Canada

Main office: Toronto

Established:
1974

Authors include:
Joseph Boyden, Kim
Echlin, Will Ferguson,
Pauline Gedge, Amitav
Ghosh, Jane Green,
Khaled Hosseini,
Stuart McLean

CEO: David Davidar

Ireland

Main office: Dublin

Established:
2002

Authors include:
Niamh Greene, Tom
Humphries, Sinéad
Moriarty, Ross O'Carroll-
Kelly, Tim Robinson

CEO: Michael McLoughlin

South Africa

Main office: Johannesburg

Established:
1989

Authors include:
Graeme Codrington,
Jennifer Crwys-Williams,
Pippa Green, Heidi Holland,
Shaun Johnson, Dalene
Matthee, Marguerite Poland,
John van de Ruit

CEO: Alison Lowry

China

Main office: Beijing

Established:
2006

Authors include:
Eileen Chang, Wang Gang,
Jiang Rong, Zhu Wen

CEO: Jo Lusby

India

Main office: New Delhi

Established:
1987

Authors include:
Ruskin Bond, Vikram
Chandra, William
Dalrymple, Shobhaa Dé,
Kiran Desai, Amitav
Ghosh, A. P. J. Abdul
Kalam, Yann Martel,
Arundhati Roy, Vikram
Seth, Khushwant Singh,
Suketu Mehta, Shashi
Tharoor

CEO: Mike Bryan

Australia

Main office: Melbourne

Established:
1946

Authors include:
Maggie Alderson,
Maggie Beer, Bryce
Courtenay, Robert Drewe,
Michael Leunig, Monica
McInerney, Rachael
Treasure, Tim Winton

CEO: Gabrielle Coyne

New Zealand

Main office: Auckland

Established:
1973

Authors include:
Alexa Johnston,
Paul Little, Peta Mathias,
Linda Olsson, Paul Sorrell,
Graham Warman

CEO: Margaret Thompson

At Penguin the relationship has grown far closer in recent years. This has nothing to do with either party being obliged to share new books or authors with the other. It has simply sprung from a better understanding of their (still quite different) needs, on the back of warmer personal ties. Editors will often consider pooling resources in joint bids, where appropriate. And, for shared authors, there is a degree of mutual support between London and New York that wise agents will now weigh carefully before assuming that transatlantic one-stop shops are snares for the unwary. There is mutual respect and goodwill on both sides that many international competitors can only envy.

Exporting books (and English)

Penguin's internationalism can also be seen in another dimension of the group's activities – its export of English-language books into the 'open' (and usually non-English) market. Taking into account titles sold from the US as well as the UK, Penguin is easily the largest exporter of English-language books, with annual revenues of more than $70 million. It is also the only large trade publisher with a single, unified global sales force. In many countries around the world, retailers are confronted with openly competing US and UK reps visiting them on behalf of the same publisher. Penguin integrates its US and UK reps into one structure. In Japan they will often make joint presentations to the major retailers. In Spain and Italy, where Penguin offices hold their own stocks, the local managers will coordinate the selling of both US and UK titles.

Wizard sales

Penguin distributed all seven volumes of Harry Potter. In India *Harry Potter and the Deathly Hallows* sold a record 265,000 copies.

There are eight sales and marketing offices around the world, with local agents employed in a wide range of other markets across Asia and eastern and central Europe. For historical reasons, the operation (with about seventy staff) is run out of London. The success of the department over many years is reflected in the Penguin sections that can be found inside book stores all over the world, from Seoul to Santiago. There has been a dramatic growth rate in US exports since 2002. Direct sales of Penguin US books into the open market have more than doubled to around $15 million, with another $15 million or so sold to international wholesalers.

企 鹅 经 典

Penguin Classics including
Alexandre Dumas's *The Three
Musketeers* and Anthony Trollope's
The Way We Live Now have been
translated into Mandarin Chinese
and Korean.

The breakdown of US sales is consistently more or less the opposite of its UK counterpart, which makes for a very effective complementarity.

The single largest market for Penguin exports from the US, by some way, is South Korea. It has a population of forty-nine million people, and most of them are seemingly preoccupied these days either with learning English or else making an entrepreneurial fortune by helping others do so. Though a fraction of China's size, the country exemplifies the fantastic opportunities that await the group, as vast numbers of people across east Asia turn to English-language books for business and for pleasure. Penguin-branded retail space is now a common feature of the book trade in Seoul – and there is every intention that it should soon become equally familiar in the giant book stores of China too.

One development that should help this along is the publication in 2008 of the first black Penguin Classics to be translated into both Korean and Mandarin Chinese, and to be published in Korea and China with local partners. The group now has a small office in Beijing, which is steadily building Penguin's presence and profile in China. China and Korea could be the template for other such businesses, in Asia and elsewhere, to which Penguin will license out its Classics texts for translation, and then provide local marketing assistance. If the group can succeed in penetrating the emerging regions of Asia as effectively as it has built a presence across Europe and Latin America, then Penguin's profile will be global by any definition.

Judge for yourself

We are lucky enough to publish some of the world's
most celebrated authors who have won their fair share
of plaudits over the years.

The Pulitzer Prize for Fiction

16 Pulitzers

2008   *The Brief Wondrous Life of
       Oscar Wao* Junot Díaz
2006   *March* Geraldine Brooks
1995   *The Stone Diaries*
       Carol Shields
1984   *Ironweed* William Kennedy
1976   *Humboldt's Gift* Saul Bellow
1972   *Angle of Repose*
       Wallace Stegner
1940   *The Grapes of Wrath*
       John Steinbeck
1930   *Laughing Boy* Oliver Lafarge
1928   *The Bridge of San Luis Rey*
       Thornton Wilder
1926   *Arrowsmith* Sinclair Lewis
1921   *The Age of Innocence*
       Edith Wharton

The Pulitzer Prize for
General Non-fiction

2005   *Ghost Wars* Steve Coll
1987   *Arab and Jew: Wounded
       Spirits in a Promised Land*
       David K. Shipler

The Pulitzer Prize for Poetry

2002   *Practical Gods* Carl Dennis
1976   *Self-Portrait in a Convex
       Mirror* John Ashbery
1952   *Collected Poems*
       Marianne Moore

The National Book Awards

22 Nationals

2005   *Europe Central*
       William Vollmann
2001   Medal for Distinguished
       Contributions to American
       Letters: Arthur Miller
2000   *In the Heart of the Sea*
       Nathaniel Philbrick
1988   *Paris Trout* Pete Dexter
1987   *Paco's Story* Larry Heinemann
1985   *White Noise* Don DeLillo
1985   *Easy in the Islands*
       Bob Shacochis
1984   *Stones for Ibarra* Harriet Doerr
1983   *The Women of Brewster Place*
       Gloria Naylor
1982   *Naming Names* Victor Navasky
1981   *The Last Cowboy* Jane Kramer
1980   *And I Worked at the Writer's
       Trade* Malcolm Cowley
1979   *The Snow Leopard*
       Peter Matthiessen
1977   *The Spectator Bird*
       Wallace Stegner
1976   *Self-Portrait in a Convex
       Mirror* John Ashbery
1976   *J.R.* William Gaddis
1975   *The Lives of a Cell*
       Lewis Thomas
1974   *Gravity's Rainbow*
       Thomas Pynchon
1971   *Mr. Sammler's Planet*
       Saul Bellow
1967   *The Fixer* Bernard Malamud
1965   *Herzog* Saul Bellow
1954   *The Adventures of Augie
       March* Saul Bellow

The Nobel Prize for Literature

25 Nobels

2003   J. M. Coetzee
1991   Nadine Gordimer
1990   Octavio Paz
1982   Gabriel García Márquez
1978   Isaac Bashevis Singer
1976   Saul Bellow
1972   Heinrich Böll
1971   Pablo Neruda
1962   John Steinbeck
1949   William Faulkner
1948   T. S. Eliot
1947   André Gide
1946   Herman Hesse
1936   Eugene O'Neill
1934   Luigi Pirandello
1933   Ivan G. Bunin
1930   Sinclair Lewis
1929   Thomas Mann
1928   Sigrid Undset
1925   George Bernard Shaw
1923   William Butler Yeats
1921   Anatole France
1920   Knut Hamsun
1913   Rabindranath Tagore
1907   Rudyard Kipling

The Man Booker Prize

10 Bookers

Penguin has published in the UK paperbacks of the following Man Booker Prize winners:

2006 *The Inheritance of Loss* Kiran Desai
1995 *The Ghost Road* Pat Barker
1992 *Sacred Hunger* Barry Unsworth
1987 *Moon Tiger* Penelope Lively
1986 *The Old Devils* Kingsley Amis
1984 *Hotel du Lac* Anita Brookner
1983 *Life & Times of Michael K* J. M. Coetzee
1976 *Saville* David Storey
1974 *The Conservationist* Nadine Gordimer
1972 *G* John Berger

The Newbery Medal

44 Newberys

Including most recently:

2005 *Al Capone Does My Shirts* Gennifer Choldenko
2001 *A Year Down Yonder* Richard Peck
1983 *Sweet Whispers, Brother Rush* Virginia Hamilton
1979 *The Westing Game* Ellen Raskin
1977 *Roll of Thunder, Hear My Cry* Mildred D. Taylor
1971 *Summer of the Swans* Betsy Byars
1953 *Secret of the Andes*

7

The best we can be

Our people and values

History and geography have intriguingly combined to ensure that Penguin is most assuredly not a collection of cookie-cutter companies. The group is more like a close federation of parties with a common agenda. Even within the same offices, this leaves room for distinct cultures (Putnam and Penguin in New York, Penguin and DK in London, and so on) to rub along in tandem. And yet... those who work in the group will nonetheless insist that every Penguin office in the world feels somehow the same. By general consent, there seems also to exist a Penguin kind of person.

Without question, there are shared values across the group that in aggregate go far to define it. Some are straightforward. They are about supporting the group's approach to publishing. There is a strong belief, for example, in the importance of producing best-of-genre books for all tastes.

Booktime

Supported by Penguin, Pearson's Booktime programme provides over 700,000 books a year for all children starting school in the UK.

Power of the PEN

Penguin supports PEN, the world's oldest human rights and literary organization, and is the sponsor of the 2009 PEN World Voices Festival in New York, which will bring together more than 100 writers from around the world.

A gain, while every large publisher pays lip service to the creed of a global marketplace, Penguin strives to work as a genuinely borderless business – insofar as this is compatible, at least, with the rights jurisdictions that survive from a distant past. There is a devotion to art and design that goes back to the earliest days of Harold Guinzburg and George Oppenheim's Viking Press, as well as to the fabled origins of the Penguin paperback. And there is a determination always to make the most of new technology, preferably in ways that will leave others looking faintly Luddite in comparison.

Habits of mind

However, if we set these matters aside to be treated as business, there remain other shared values that are more about habits of mind. They are ways of thinking about people and ideas that are taken for granted at Penguin. DK Eyewitness Travel is unlikely ever to want to package them as a 'Top 10', but in this chapter are ten for consideration (in absolutely no logical order).

I t is a daunting list. Any working environment that lives up to these values, one might suppose, would be hard to leave. So it comes as no surprise to find that Penguin's senior ranks are indeed full of people who have been with the company virtually all their working lives. This longevity among so many senior staff brings a sense of stability, loyalty and continuity to Penguin that is unmistakeably a seminal feature of the group. It would be wrong, and rather depressing, to characterize longevity as a value in itself, but it is strong evidence that all those other values are more than pious aspirations. The business buys into them and many of them form the very basis upon which Penguin was created...

'We have enjoyed the best and happiest years of the firm. What we have to do is to see that the principles on which it was founded are maintained into the foreseeable future.'
Sir Allen Lane *(1902 – 70)*

1. Ideas first, the rest to follow

The group aspires to a workplace culture that lets individuals run with their own ideas. It provides the organizational back-up to square these with commercial reality, but the ideas get top billing. The best stories generally revolve around individuals who have come up with the unexpected.

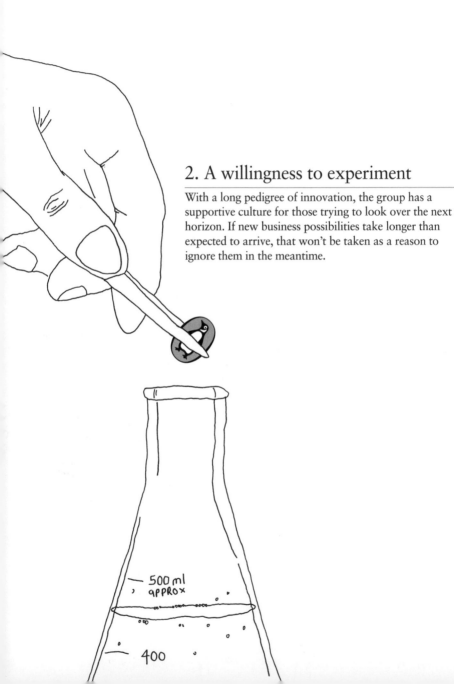

2. A willingness to experiment

With a long pedigree of innovation, the group has a supportive culture for those trying to look over the next horizon. If new business possibilities take longer than expected to arrive, that won't be taken as a reason to ignore them in the meantime.

3. Trust in the individual

Considering the professional rigour with which most of its activities are tracked within a disciplined business process, people at Penguin enjoy a remarkably unstructured environment. Individuals are given a lot of autonomy to decide their own priorities.

4. Awareness of the environment

There is a real commitment to green causes all across the group. This isn't a corporate mantra, but a grassroots movement which sees employees across the globe united in their efforts to reduce Penguin's impact on the environment, from the small (installing motion sensors for lights) to the slightly grander (a 96-acre, 40,000-tree Penguin wood in the UK, and a co-branded campaign with the Nature Conservancy in the US to back the planting of a billion new trees in Brazil's Atlantic Forest).

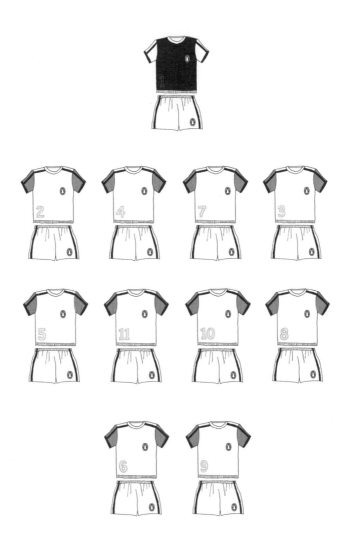

5. Collegiality and teamwork

Publishing is emphatically a team-based activity. Penguin draws huge strength from making teamwork a big priority and good working relations reach all the way through the publishing process.

6. Hard-headed commercialism

While employees can indulge their love of books, the nature of the work is strictly unsentimental. All are made aware of commercial goals and financial objectives, not to the point of distraction but just enough to ensure that market realities are never far from employees' minds.

7. Valuing the individual

Penguin takes its cue here from Pearson, the parent
company that sets great store by treating employees
decently. No one joins Penguin to get rich, but there
are plenty of benefits that help make the lifestyle as
congenial as possible.

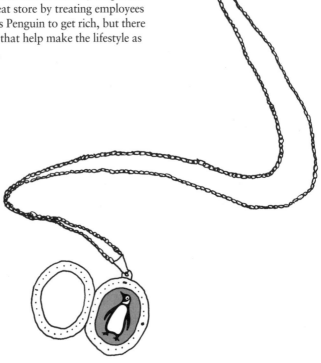

8. Courage and integrity

If a book is judged worth publishing, there's a deep-
rooted antipathy at Penguin to the idea of not publishing
in the interests of a quiet life. Sometimes matters are
resolved relatively speedily but other battles, such as
the libel suit against historian David Irving in 2000,
are more costly and protracted.

9. A shared purpose

While commercial reality is the driving force, there is also a shared conviction at Penguin that books – in all their many genres – really can change people's lives. The group provides financial and in-kind support to a wide range of literacy programmes around the world.

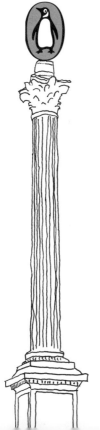

10. Pride in the past

Nothing to do with resting on laurels, this is about acknowledging that 'what's past is prologue'. For today's employees, Penguin's heritage links the work they do with the legacy of those before, as it will too for those who come after. And that's the crux: people who are lucky enough to work at Penguin know that they are passing through, as it were, and so must see themselves ultimately as custodians of the brand.

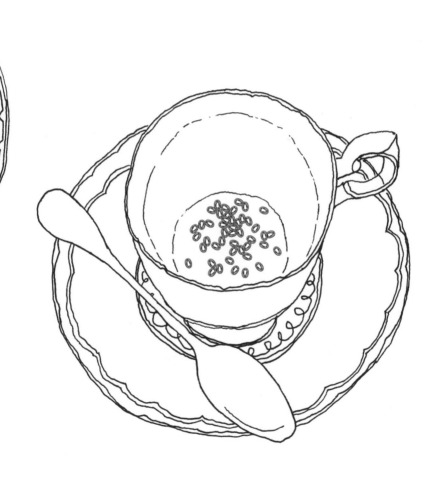

8
What next?
Preparing for the future

I t was the New York Yankees manager Yogi Berra who
memorably said he never made predictions – especially
about the future. Penguin doesn't make them either.
But its appetite for change goes a long way beyond
making contingency arrangements. There are people
in every corner of the group busily working on the new
opportunities being opened up by digitization. Some in the
industry fear the prospect of a tsunami that might sweep away
the economics of the traditional publishing industry. You don't
hear much of that kind of talk at Penguin. There's a palpable
excitement around the place that new business models are
shaping up, in a way that hasn't happened since... well, to
pick a date, 1935.

But you don't need to go back to the invention of the
paperback to find Penguin leading the way on new ideas.
It was the first trade publisher into audiobooks and eBooks,
the first with its own website and official blog, and the first
to create an online community.

Penguin worldwide websites

Around 15 million people
visited Penguin websites around
the world in 2008.

traveldk.com

DK's award-winning website
allows visitors to assemble their
own tailored travel guide.

Setting aside Harry Potter's, which would hardly be a fair comparison, Penguin's websites are the most visited in the world of books by a country mile – they have around fifteen million visitors a year, and that's not counting traffic on the Chinese/English site launched by Penguin China in August 2007.

As these online firsts suggest, the internet looks like being at least as disruptive a force in the industry in the years ahead as Penguin's arrival on the scene in 1935 ever was. Digital technology is transforming the industry, not just by offering new formats and platforms for content, but also by creating new channels of distribution and the opportunity to reform the entire publishing process. Penguin has appointed a group digital director, Genevieve Shore, and has set up a Digital Business Council, which has been drawing people together from all over the group since the beginning of 2008. And while it is their job to make sure the opportunities that the digital world offers are properly exploited, it is down to everyone across all parts of the company to engage with them – an obligation keenly accepted across the group.

While some of the internet's changes will be gradual, others have had a more immediate effect. Take marketing, for example, where the internet has been enriching Penguin's activities for years. Most obviously, it provides a shop window for Penguin itself and for Penguin books of all kinds. Anyone with a love of books can spend hours wandering around Penguin's online frontlists and catalogued archives. And if they want something a little more free-range than the official website, there are plenty of other places, from Wikipedia and the blogosphere to YouTube, Facebook and MySpace ('Penguin, 73 years old, London, UK'), where they can find Penguin-linked news and events. All this has transformed the marketing of new titles, especially to teenagers and young adults.

Of course, the internet is much more than just a medium for marketing, and it will start attracting some readers for whom online products themselves have an edge over physical books. Nowhere is this more apparent, as we have already noted, than in DK and Travel publishing. But other divisions, too, have begun exploring this uncharted territory.

In one of many experiments, for example, readers have been invited to write a story from scratch in a 'wiki-novel' called *A Million Penguins*. It may be the first novel in history with more writers than readers – and no one at Penguin would claim it's a good read – but the value was always seen to lie in the process rather than in the end product. And this reveals something fundamentally important about Penguin's culture which is well aligned with the digital world: a willingness to experiment without the certainty of an immediate return.

There are many other examples of this innovative spirit. Penguin US partnered with Amazon on a breakthrough novel award, for instance, which invited new writers to submit manuscripts online. After these had been reviewed and shortlisted by Penguin editors, a winner was chosen by Amazon readers and awarded a publishing contract with Penguin. (Fortunately, the award's designers put a cap on the submissions so that only the first 5,000 entries were accepted. The group's editors would otherwise probably still be reading through the manuscripts that winged their way in.) Penguin UK, meanwhile, has launched its award-winning 'blog a Penguin' initiative. All of the 1,300 Penguin Classics were sent out to readers, who then posted their own reviews and conversed with fellow readers on the official Classics blog.

puffin.co.uk

The recently re-launched Puffin website invites readers to meet their favourite authors and illustrators, take a sneaky peek around their studios, listen to podcasts and play games in the Puffin playground.

penguin.com.cn

Penguin was the first English-language trade publisher to launch a Chinese-language website.

What's next in text.

Penguin is also offering a helping hand to its authors, as they come to terms with the need for their own websites, blogs and podcasts. In New York and London, authors have been issued a guide, *Penguin Authors Guide to Online Marketing*. ('Online marketing alone won't guarantee that your book is a success. But by becoming part of the online conversation – and giving readers the chance to discuss you and your book – it at least gives you the opportunity to compete.')

As Penguin looks for ways to reach out to new readers via new formats and new channels, it does so with a constant eye on how to maximize opportunities for its authors and illustrators while protecting their intellectual property. To this end, Penguin and four other leading publishers, including sister company Pearson Education, have reached a landmark agreement with Google that sees the creation of a 'Rights Registry'. Funded by Google, the registry will compensate owners of intellectual property for

File   Edit   View   History   Bookmarks   Tools

http://www

Home   **Books**   **Events**   **Competitions**

Search

spinebreakers

spinebreakers.co.uk Launched in September 2007, Spinebreakers is Penguin's pioneering online book community run by teenagers, for teenagers.

Spinebreaker (n)

Any story-surfing, web-expl
ord-loving, day-dreaming,
tist/ thinker aged

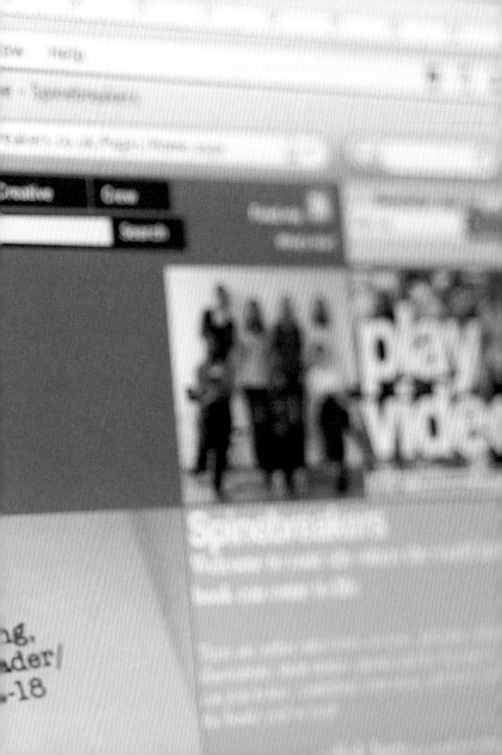

online access to their works. This will open the way to new business models for the sale and distribution of content, broadening the audience for books while protecting authors' copyrights. The book industry may still be struggling to fully come to terms with the digital age, but at least a start has been made.

A new breed of readers

Though still accounting for only a tiny percentage of publishing revenues, eBooks tend to figure prominently in the headlines. The US has led the way with the launch of the first generation of eReaders, including Sony's *eReader* and Amazon's Kindle. Penguin's eBook revenues are rising exponentially, albeit from a small base. Contrary to what you might think, eBooks aren't just for techno-geeks. Middle-aged women are the biggest buyers, and the bestselling titles are the hottest books in women's romance.

The group is hard at work converting backlist titles for the new channel – a single book currently takes around five weeks to digitize – while adjusting to a different era in which new books will be published in hard copy and digital form simultaneously. Penguin UK published its first dual-format titles in September 2008. Hopes are high that, for the first time in many years, the book market might now be poised for some growth in absolute terms. There is also the prospect of selling eBooks in the emerging markets of Asia, where it is not hard to imagine how eReaders in remote places could leapfrog the economics of a barely nascent retail book trade. But turning eBook dreams into reality is going to involve some tricky economics in the Western world too.

Penguin mobile

Penguin has become the first book publisher to develop an iPhone application that will allow readers to enjoy Penguin content and news on their iPhone.

Pride (and prejudice) in technology

Penguin's enriched eBook Classics invite readers to go beyond the pages of popular works, and gain more insight into the life and times of an author and the period in which the book was originally written, creating a rich reading experience.

Jamie's Ministry of Food

For the launch of Jamie Oliver's latest book, Penguin developed a multi-destination online campaign in collaboration with MySpace, inviting people to take part in his 'Pass it on' recipe-sharing campaign.

There will be pricing issues, most immediately, which will pose an acute challenge for every publisher: given the start-up costs of digitization, and the unrelenting pressure on the retail prices of ordinary books, treating eBooks as a cheap alternative will hardly be feasible for the industry. Penguin sees the digital medium not as a cut-price option, but as an opportunity to provide an entirely new reading experience.

The group's Enriched eBook Classics, for example, will do what the label says. (Jane Austen's *Pride and Prejudice* will include period recipes and commentaries on early-nineteenth-century English social etiquette, among other digital features.) Authors will need to be properly compensated for the electronic publication of their work – and the issue of copyright territoriality will need to be addressed.

Perhaps, with clever technology, ways will be found to reconcile traditional territorial arrangements with the borderless world of the internet. Or perhaps we are just at the start of a digital era which will sweep away much that has been a familiar part of publishing for decades past. Whatever the future, leadership within the industry will surely lie with those who take the most creative line in bringing writers and readers together. Penguin will go on seeking to set the pace across the board – taking its digital chances, certainly, but doing everything possible at the same time to reinforce the bookishness of books.

Afterword

We didn't design *The Book of Penguin* to be *comprehensive*, either as a history of the company, a description of what we do now or as a guide to the future. So if you're thinking, 'I just can't believe they didn't mention so and so', please accept our apologies. We wanted instead to sketch a portrait of an organization that feels different and, as I said in my introduction, *important* to those of us who are connected with Penguin in one way or another.

Organizations age, just like people, so not every detail of the Penguin described in this book will be recognizable five years from now. But I would be astonished if the character and values of the company had changed. We'll still be obsessive about the quality of what we publish, and the professionalism with which we go about our business. We'll want to be brave, imaginative and decent in everything we do. We'll be publishing new kinds of content, on new platforms, in new markets. And we'll still be manufacturing millions of that centuries-old artefact: the book.

Acknowledgements I want to say a few words of thanks to the people outside Penguin who helped to make this happen.

Duncan Campbell-Smith, who worked at Penguin way back when, is the author of the book. He spent hours in conversation with many people, most of whom still work at Penguin, about this great company and what it means to them. He then applied his formidable energy and intelligence to the challenge of shaping those impressions into a simple story.

We also asked the designers at Radley Yeldar to create a style for the book that matched the quality of our design heritage, and reflected both the flippant and serious sides of our personality.

Every reader will have his or her own view, but I think Duncan and Radley Yeldar succeeded magnificently, and I thank them both.

John Makinson *Chairman and CEO, Penguin Group*